By Neil Howe & William Strauss
www.lifecourse.com/college

# Millennials
# Go to College

**STRATEGIES FOR A NEW GENERATION ON CAMPUS:**
RECRUITING AND ADMISSIONS, CAMPUS LIFE, AND THE CLASSROOM

# Millennials
## Go to College

Howe, Neil and Strauss, William
    Millenials go to college

ISBN 1-578-58033-1

Library of Congress Control Number 2002117476

The American Association of Collegiate Registrars
and Admissions Officers (AACRAO), founded in 1910,
is a nonprofit, voluntary, professional, association of
more than 9,400 higher education admission and
registration professionals who represent nearly 2,500
institutions and agencies in the United States and in
28 countries around the world. The mission of the
association is to provide leadership in policy initia-
tion, interpretation, and implememtation in the
global education community. This is accomplished
through the identification and promotion of standards and best practices in enrollment management,
information technology, instructional management,
and student services. AACRAO members are primarily registrars, admissions officers, and enrollment
managers, as well as other professionals in related
enrollment offices.

# *Table of Contents*

The Millennial Generation has long interested us for personal as well as professional reasons. We are each the parent of two, in both cases a boy and girl, age 8 and 11 (Howe), 18 and 19 (Strauss).

We've been studying their generation since the days of its first preschoolers, back in the middle 1980s. When we wrote *Generations*, over a dozen years ago, we described how the children then entering elementary school rode "a powerful crest of protective concern," how they were seen as "precious" by Boomer parents who wielded a "perfectionist approach to child nurture" in an adult world that was "rediscovering an affection and sense of responsibility for other people's children."

In 1990, when most youth assessments were downbeat, even grim, we forecast that as these new children passed through adolescence "substance abuse, crime, suicide, unwed pregnancy will all decline." We made similar predictions for teen employment and television viewing.

When these trends all came to pass, we were not surprised. There are good reasons, rooted in how they were raised and in the rhythms of history, for why this occurred.

Again and again over the centuries, in America and elsewhere, new generations arise that both correct the trends set in motion by their parents and fill the role being vacated by their grandparents. It is happening again. That's what these leading-edge Millennials are doing with (and to) a "Boomer Generation" in midlife and a "G.I. Generation" deep in elderhood.

Two years ago, when we published *Millennials Rising*, we chose as a subtitle "The Next Great Generation"—partly because, as a group, they exhibit qualities not generally seen in American youth since today's "senior citizens"—who, as collegians, back in the 1920s and '30s, were similarly confident, optimistic, team oriented, rule following, and eager to achieve. And, just as today's elder Americans did in their own youth, Millennials are growing up seeing their needs and dreams climb to the top of the national agenda.

We wrote *Millennials Go To College* at the urging of many college administrators, deans, registrars, admissions officers, and faculty members who, after having read our books or heard our lectures, agreed with us that Millennials are in fact arriving—and have asked us what they should do.

In Part One, we summarize the basic facts about today's new collegiate generation. We explain its location in history in relation to older generations. We describe the seven core Millennial traits: *special, sheltered, confident, team-oriented, conventional, pressured,* and *achieving.*

In Part Two, we explain what each of these traits means for colleges and universities—for recruiting and admissions, campus life, and the classroom—and what awaits in the years ahead, in career counseling, graduate school, the alumni ranks, and the world at large.

By necessity, we can only cover so much ground here. For readers who wish to learn more, we recommend *Millennials Rising* (2000), which we published just as the much-celebrated high school "Class of 2000" was entering college.

If you would like to learn more about our historical method, would like to see what we've written about Millennials in earlier years, or would like to pursue your own research on generational topics, please see *Generations* (1991) and *The Fourth Turning* (1997). To see what we wrote about Gen Xers when they were collegians and young adults, please see *13th-Gen* (1993), which we published when today's 30-year-olds were still in college.

We invite readers with comments or questions to contact us, at authors@lifecourse.com.

One thing you notice, when you study the students who pass through educational institutions as a succession of generations, is how each generation trains the next in skills and values—and how, in so doing, each makes a profound contribution to the ongoing march of civilization. From the time when Benjamin Franklin's generation taught Thomas Jefferson's, through the time when Woodrow Wilson's taught Franklin Roosevelt's, on to our own childhood when the best and brightest Rosie the Riveters taught us, we can see how tightly the chain of human progress is tied to the teaching and learning of the arts and sciences.

The questions, "Why do we teach? What is education for?" are best answered when you view the current generation of students as future parents, scientists, generals, playwrights, leaders, artists, historians—and teachers. When we describe Millennials as a "next great generation," we speak not just of their ancestry but also of their destiny.

Whatever that destiny may be, these young people will someday look back and thank you, their educators, for the gifts you gave them that made it possible.


William Strauss
Neil Howe
October, 2002

# 1 | A New Generation Goes to College

"Meet the Millennials, and rejoice."

— ANNA QUINDLEN, NEWSWEEK (2000)

# A New Generation
# Goes to College

A new generational wave is breaking across campuses in America.

Dating back to its first births, in the early 1980s, you could see this Millennial Generation coming. Everywhere these boys and girls have been, from bulging nurseries to the new "Baby on Board" minivans, from day-care center to kindergarten through high school, they have changed the face of youth—and transformed every institution they've touched.

Now the first Millennials are in college, along with their intrusive parents—and the glare of the media. At this writing, these young women and men are in their junior year. Soon, they'll start entering graduate and professional schools.

The years ahead can be a new golden age for America's colleges and universities. So too will they be years of increased stress, scrutiny, security, accountability, tuition relief, and—very likely—mainstream political activism of a kind that will seem oddly unfamiliar to most veteran Boomer activists.

It will not be an easy time. The nature of every college function from admissions to campus life to the classroom to career counseling will change dramatically. The doctrine of *in loco parentis*, thrown over by rebellious Boomers forty years ago, will reemerge in a new community guise as the Boomers' own children fill dorm rooms.

The pressure on resources will be enormous. During the Gen X collegiate era of the 1980s and '90s, admissions were stable and costs controllable, tuitions and endowments rising. Students hunkered down, their fringes more powerful than their core, on the whole attracting little public attention. During the upcoming Millennial collegiate era, through the remainder of this decade and the one to follow, admissions will be more volatile and costs more unpredictable, tuitions more restrained (and price competition flagrant), and endowments less reliable. The core of students will overpower the fringes, and as a group, they will command far more public attention.

Millennials are smart, ambitious, incredibly busy, very ethnically diverse, and dominated by girls, to this point. They make decisions jointly with parents ("copurchasing" a college) and believe in big brands (with "reputation" counting for a lot). And they are very numerous, very intent on going to college, and have very demanding parents.

Through the coming decade, they will transform the university world as profoundly as the Boomers did in the 1960s—but in very different, even opposite, ways. As happened in the '60s, some universities will figure out the new generation, deal with it correctly, and rise in reputation—and others will not. Some universities will make wise budget decisions, deftly tailoring income and expenditure streams around the needs and tastes of the new generation—and others will not. Some will market their college product smartly to the new youth mindset, and to the new parental mindset—and others will not.

The next two decades may well become one of those occasional eras when the rise of a new generation coincides with turbulent global events to elevate the role of higher education in preparing the nation's "best and brightest" and in laying out the blueprint for a better future. The last comparable era was the 1930s and 1940s, decades when the collegiate pecking order was reshuffled. It was through the war-winning collegians of those years that the enduring reputations of many of today's elite institutions were forged.

The stakes are just as high in this Millennial era. Colleges and universities that figure out the new trends, make wise tuition and budget choices, and market intelligently to today's youth, will be able to "re-brand" their own reputations, leapfrog rivals—and, perhaps, join the top echelons of academe. And, in this coming era of accountability, those that do not could fall in reputation, or worse.

Wherever you are in university life, you face a choice. You can ignore this breaking Millennial wave, by treating today's collegians as you did the last generation. You can resist it, by pursuing decades-old agendas. You can ride it, by adapting as fast as you can to new needs as they arise. Or you can *lead* this new youth wave, by preparing for Millennials before they arrive in full force.

Change is in the air on today's college campuses.

In some ways, these are boom times for academia. Applications are way up, and many schools are finding they can become much more selective. But its also a time of spreading uncertainty and unease. Colleges and universities find themselves spending more and more on public relations, mindful of how much their reputations and rankings seem to be in flux. The new students strike many faculty members as well-prepared and unexpectedly eager to please, but also as pressured and reluctant to take creative chances. Every little controversy—a case of alcohol poisoning in a frat house, a professor who criticizes the War on Terrorism, a T.A. who is seen dating a student, an admissions department found to be using a quota or asking other schools about their scholarships—gets the white hot glare of national media attention.

What's going on here? Very simple. A new generation—the Millennial Generation—is coming of college age.

Since infancy, this generation has been the object of intense parental and societal attention, in forms as diverse as "zero tolerance" drug rules to a powerful school reform movement to whole new areas of pro-child health, safety, and "values education" initiatives. Largely as a result of that attention, this generation is marked by character traits that separate it from Generation X. Many of these traits are positive. These youths are confident and optimistic, they are team- and rule-oriented, and they work very hard. Rates of tobacco and alcohol use, violent crime, out-of-wedlock pregnancies, and suicide rates all are way down among today's teenagers, while SAT scores have been rising steadily.

To be sure, all of these positive traits also have their shadow side. Along with a greater willingness to play by the rules comes a new tendency to conformity. Along with high confidence, and a feeling of preciousness, comes a tendency to risk aversion. Along with an elevated respect for institutions come high expectations of authority and "zero tolerance" for institutional failure—an attitude that this generation will apply with particular force to institutions of higher learning.

In many ways that please older Americans, and in some that don't, Millennials are recasting the youth mood in America. For colleges and universities, this promises to be an era in which reputations are rapidly reshuffled. Colleges and universities that seize the opportunity will thrive and, perhaps, elevate in rank. Others may soon find themselves embarrassingly—even dangerously—at odds with students, parents, alumni, politicians, regulators, the courts, and the media.

The arrival of young Millennials in the decade of the 2000s will trigger social and political consequences that could be as profound as (though profoundly different from) those triggered by young Boomers in the 1960s.

To understand how and why this may be true, let's first ask:
*Who are they?*

# Part One

# 2 | Meet the Millennials

"The Millennials, the first batch of which
are the high-school class of 2000,…are,
as a group, pleasant, cheerful, helpful,
ambitious, and community-oriented."

— MARY ANN JOHNSON, FILM CRITIC (2000)

# Meet the Millennials

Meet the new students. "It's very rare to get a student to challenge anything or to take a position that's counter to what the professor says. They are disconcertingly comfortable with authority," says Princeton sociologist Robert Wurthnow of today's new crop of college freshmen. "They're eager to please, eager to jump through whatever hoops the faculty puts in front of them, eager to conform."

And, meet the new moms and dads—whom Wake Forest official Mary Gerardy aptly describes as "helicopter parents," always hovering—ultra-protective, unwilling to let go, enlisting "the team" (physician, lawyer, psychiatrist, professional counselors) to assert a variety of special needs and interests.

Where once parents simply unloaded the station wagon at the start of orientation week, kissed good-bye and drove home, now they linger for days—fussing, meddling, tearing, and even ranting if they think their very special child isn't getting the very best of everything. When they don't get their way, they threaten to take their business elsewhere or sue.

**2002 Program Titles for Freshmen Parent Orientation**

*What Have You Done With My Child?*
– University of North Carolina at Wilmington

*May They Follow Your Path and Not Your Footsteps*
– Ohio Northern University

*Between Mothering and Smothering, Between Fathering and Bothering*
– University of Southern California

## The Changing Face of Youth

Teachers, professors, military officers, and others who work with youth often pride themselves on being the first to notice generational change when it occurs. Yet even those in closest contact with the youth culture are sometimes confounded by both the direction and timing of such change. Usually, the mistake is to assume that next year's collegians will be like last year's, only a bit more so. Most of the time that's true, but every two decades or so such linear projections prove to be catastrophically mistaken.

Consider the following expectations for a new batch of youth at various times during the postwar era:

### The Silent Generation came as a surprise.

In 1946, about the time General George Marshall declared the nation's victorious troops to be "the best damn kids in the world," Americans braced for fresh ranks of organized collegians who would take the mass mobilizations of the New Deal and World War II to a higher level of activism. These new youths were expected to be just like the world-conquering generation just before them, different only in that they might carry familiar youth traits to a higher level.

This didn't happen. After the returning G.I.s flowed quickly into and then out of the nation's campuses, everyone was surprised to learn that the next generation of "teenagers" seemed uninterested in conquering the world. They kept their heads down, worried about their "permanent records," and planned on early marriages and long careers with big organizations.

Rather than change the system, the new collegians wanted to work within it. Looking back, historian William Manchester wrote, "[N]ever had American youth been so withdrawn, cautious, unimaginative, indifferent, unadventurous—and silent...They waited so patiently for everything that visitors to college campuses began commenting on their docility."

### Boomers came as a surprise.

By the early 1960s, Americans had grown used to talking about a "Silent Generation" of college students. As experts looked ahead to the onrushing bulge of children known as the "baby boom" who were about to arrive at college, they foresaw a new corps of technocratic corporatists, a Silent Generation to the next degree, even more pliable and conformist than the gray flannel "lonely crowd" right before them. "Employers are going to love this generation," Cal-Berkeley's Clark Kerr declared in 1959, "They are going to be easy to handle. There aren't going to be any riots."

Events, to say the least, turned out otherwise. Remarkably, not even the biggest-name social scientists—not even Erik Erikson or Margaret Mead—saw a hint of the youth explosion that was about to shake America.

### Generation X came as a surprise.

Let's move forward another 20 years. Around 1980, experts in youth fields accepted the Boomers as the new norm for adolescent attitudes and behavior. The question was soon raised: What, they asked, would come from the next crop? These were the "Baby Busters" who had no memories of the assassination of John Kennedy and no clear impression of Woodstock, Vietnam, or even Watergate. What would they be like? Once again, the expectation was linear, that these youths would be like Boomers, only more so. Demographic forecasters suggested that the teens in the 1980s and 1990s would be more ideological, "holistic," and morals-driven—extending what *American Demographics* termed "an ongoing trend away from material aspirations toward non-materialistic goals."

Those predictions were rudely overturned when the scrappy, pragmatic, and free-agent Gen X persona emerged a few years later. Disco gave way to MTV, soul to hip hop, Robin Williams to Tom Cruise. Long-haired ideologues were replaced by raging, Mohawked punks, suicidal grunge stars, goateed gamers, professional soldiers, gangsta rappers, and business school "power tools." The journey was no longer the reward; instead winning was "the only thing." College professors were confronted with students whose most piercing question seemed to be, "Is this on the test?" rather than "Is this relevant?" Once again, institutions that serve youth—from colleges to employers to the armed services—were thrown into disarray.

*Millennials are coming as a surprise.*

Today, another 20 years have passed, and yet another generational change is on the doorstep. As a group, Millennials are unlike any other youths in living memory. They are more numerous, more affluent, better educated, and more ethnically diverse. More important, they are beginning to manifest a wide array of positive social habits that older Americans no longer associate with youth, including a new focus on teamwork, achievement, modesty, and good conduct.

Yet most people's perception of youth (especially those who don't have regular contact with teens) still lags behind reality. As was true 20, 40, and 60 years ago, a common adult view is that today's teens are like the prior batch (Generation X), taken to the next degree (alias, Gen "Y"). A study recently published in the academic journal, *Social Policy Research*, finds American adults take a dim view of the younger generation. Among the findings:

* Only 16 percent of adult Americans agree that people under the age of 30 share most of their moral and ethical values.

* Confronted with what was presented as a "true news story" about recent trends among teenagers, adults consistently overlooked the positive data (which dominated the story) and focused instead on the few negative trends.

* The three most frequently reported topics of youth news on the local stations are crime victimization, accidents involving young people, and violent juvenile crime, accounting for nearly half of all youth coverage. Five other frequently reported topics were: property crimes committed by juveniles, domestic violence or sexual abuse, alcohol abuse, and individual health problems.

These findings are typical. Noting the tiny percentage of adult Americans who believe that young people share their values, public opinion analyst Meg Bostrom observes: "In the eyes of adults, this puts young people's values above only those of homosexuals, welfare recipients, and rich people." To believe the newspapers, you'd suppose America's schools are full of teenagers who can't read in the classroom, shoot one another in the hallways, spend their loose change on tongue rings, and couldn't care less who runs the country.

Part of this phenomenon is due to what David Whitman calls the rising "optimism gap" of the 1990s. That is the tendency of people to be positive about their own lives and families (and the young people they know personally) while being very negative about the state of America in general (and youth in general). When asked about their parenting skills, parents give themselves an A or B—but give all other parents a D or F.

How depressing. And how wrong.

Look closely at youth indicators, and you'll see that attitudes and behaviors among today's youth represent a sharp break from Generation X, and are running exactly counter to trends launched by the Boomers. Across the board, Millennials are challenging the dominant and negative stereotype.

Are they pessimists? No. They're optimists. Nine in ten describe themselves as "happy," "confident," and "positive." Teen suicide rates are declining for the first time in the post-war era. A rapidly decreasing share of teenagers worry about violence, sex, or drugs, and a rapidly increasing share say that growing up is easier for them than it was for their parents.

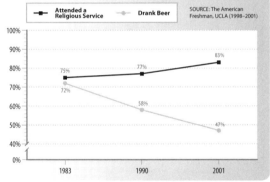

◄ Figure 1

National U.S. Freshmen Survey, Activities Done at Least "Occasionally" in the Past Year

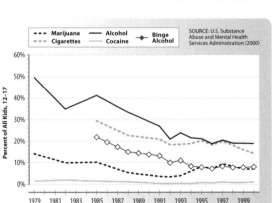

◄ Figure 2

Share of Kids Aged 12–17 having Specified Drug within Last Month, 1979 to 2000

Are they rule-breakers? No. They're rule-followers. Over the past ten years, rates of violent crime among teens has fallen by 70 percent, rates of teen pregnancy and abortion by 30 percent, rates of high-school sexual activity by 20 percent, and rates of alcohol and tobacco consumption are reaching all-time lows. As public attention to school shootings has risen, their actual incidence has fallen. Even including such shootings as Columbine, there have been fewer than half as many killings by students since 1998 (averaging fewer than 15 per year) as there were in the early 1990s (over 40 per year).

Are they self-absorbed? No. From school uniforms to team learning and team grading, they are gravitating toward group activity. Twenty years ago, "community service" was unheard of in most high schools. Today, it is the norm. According to a 1999 Roper survey, more teenagers blamed "selfishness" than anything else when asked about "the major cause of problems in this country."

**Figure 3 ▶**

Suicide Rate for Youth Aged 15–19 and 20–24, 1970 to 2000

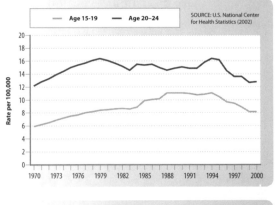

Are they distrustful? No. They accept authority. Most teens say they identify with their parents' values, and more than nine in ten say they "trust" and "feel close to" their parents. Half say they trust gov-

**Figure 4 ▶**

Serious Violent Crime*, Rate of Offenders and Victims Aged 12–17, 1980 to 2001

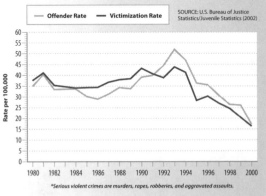

ernment to do what's right all or most of the time—twice the share of older people answering the same question in the same poll. Large majorities of teens favor tougher rules against misbehavior in the classroom and society at large.

Are they neglected? No. They're the most watched-over generation in memory. The typical day of a child, tween, or teen has become a nonstop round of parents, relatives, teachers, coaches, babysitters, counselors, chaperones, minivans, surveillance cams, and curfews. Since the mid-1980s, "unstructured activity" has been the most rapidly declining use of time among preteens.

Are they stupid? No. During the 1990s, aptitude test scores have risen within every racial and ethnic group, espe-

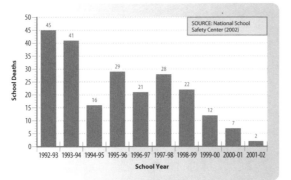

◀ **Figure 5**

Annual Number of Killings by Students, Grades K–12, at All U.S. Schools, 1992 to 2002

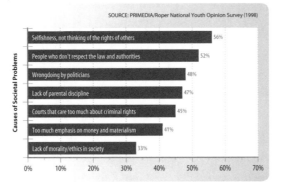

◀ **Figure 6**

Major causes of problems in society today— top seven answers from students in grades 7–12 in 1998

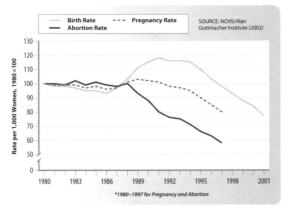

◀ **Figure 7**

Rates of Pregnancy, Abortion, and Birth for Girls Aged 15–17, 1980 to 2000*

cially in elementary schools. Eight in ten teenagers say it's "cool to be smart," while a record share of teenagers say they "look forward to school," take advanced placement tests, and plan to attend college.

Are they another "lost" generation? No. The better word is "found." Born in an era when Americans showed a more positive attitude toward children,

Figure 8 ▶

Total Number of
Students Enrolled in
U.S. Institutions of
Higher Learning,
1975 to 2010

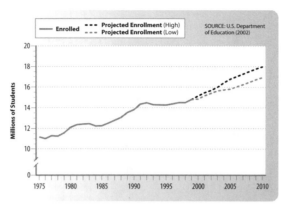

the Millennials are the product of a birthrate reversal. During the Gen Xer childhood, planned parenting meant contraceptives; during the Millennial childhood, it has meant visits to the fertility clinic. In 1998, the number of u.s. children surged past its previous Baby-Boom peak, and over the next decade, college freshmen enrollment is due to grow by roughly 40,000 per year.

## Generational Location in History

One way to define a generation's location in history is to think of a turning point in the national memory that its earliest birth cohorts just missed. Boomers, for example, are the generation whose eldest members have no memory of VJ Day. Gen Xers are the generation whose eldest members have no memory of John Kennedy's assassination. Millennials are the generation whose eldest members have no memory of sitting in school watching the space shuttle Challenger disintegrate.

Let's trace the historical location of each of the prior generations described earlier.

The Silent arrived during the Great Depression and World War II, events they witnessed through the eyes of childhood, tending their Victory Gardens, while the next-older (G.I.) generation built and sailed in the Victory Ships that won the war.

Boomers arrived during the "Great American High" that followed the war, a childhood era of warmth and indulgence that marked them forever as a "postwar" generation, while the next-older Silent compliantly entered the suburban and corporate world.

Gen Xers arrived during the "Consciousness Revolution," amid the cultural turbulence of the Boomers' young adulthood.

# Six U.S. Generations and Nearly 120 Birth Years

Except for many Boomers (who assume they've got the landscape mapped), when you talk generations, the first thing most folks want to know is: Where do I fit? This table puts the Millennials, and their five predecessor generations, into perspective. Think about your own family—your parents, your favorite aunt or uncle, your youngest brother, your great-grandmother. When were they born, and how did their generational membership shape them? Then think about some individuals who've inspired you—movie stars, great writers, even political leaders—and speculate whether they have ended up carrying out a key part of their own generation's "script."

**The Lost Generation** (Born 1883–1900) had to grow up fast—amidst urban blight, unregulated drug use, "sweat shop" child labor, and massive immigration. As children, their violence, independence, and low educational achievement worried parents. As twentysomethings, they were brassy flappers, union scabs, expatriate novelists, and nihilist "flaming youth." They also pioneered entire economic sectors—supermarkets, roadside commerce, radio and aviation—we take for granted today. After surviving a Great Depression that hit during their peak earning years, they slowed down and, during World War Two, delivered pugnacious midlife leadership. As crusty "Norman Rockwell" elders, they distrusted public power, gave generously to their world-conquering juniors, and asked remarkably little for themselves. *Louis Armstrong, Irving Berlin, William Boeing, Al Capone, Raymond Chandler, Amelia Earhart, Ernest Hemingway, the Marx Brothers, Dorothy Parker, George Patton, Harry Truman, Mae West.*

**The G.I. Generation** (Born 1901–24) enjoyed a "good kid" reputation as the beneficiaries of new playgrounds, scouting clubs, vitamins, and child-labor restrictions. They came of age with the sharpest rise in schooling ever recorded. As young adults, their uniformed corps patiently endured Depression and heroically conquered foreign enemies. In a midlife subsidized by the G.I. Bill, they built suburbs, invented vaccines, plugged missile gaps, and launched moon rockets. Their unprecedented grip on the Presidency (1961 through '92) began with the New Frontier, Great Society, and Model Cities, but wore down through Vietnam, Watergate, and budget deficits. As senior citizens, they safeguarded their "entitlements" but had little influence over culture and values. *Hazel Bishop, Doris Day, Walt Disney, Judy Garland, Alex Haley, John Kennedy, Ray Kroc, Ann Landers, Charles Lindbergh, Claire Booth Luce, Ronald Reagan, John Steinbeck.*

**The Silent Generation** (Born 1925–42) grew up as the suffocated children of war and Depression. They came of age just too late to be war heroes and just too early to be youthful free spirits. Instead, this early marrying "lonely crowd" became the risk-averse technicians and professionals as well as the sensitive rock 'n' rollers and civil rights advocates of a post-Crisis era in which conformity seemed to be a sure ticket to success. Midlife was an anxious "passage" for a generation torn between stolid elders and passionate juniors. Their surge to power coincided with fragmenting families, cultural diversity, institutional complexity, and too much litigation. They are entering elderhood with unprecedented affluence, a hip style, and a reputation for indecision. *Shirley Temple, Bill Cosby, Nora Ephron, Martin Luther King Jr., Richard Cheney, Sandra Day O'Connor, Rod Serling, Paul Simon, Colin Powell, Alvin Toffler, Gloria Steinem.*

**The Boom Generation** (Born 1943–60) grew up as indulged youth during an era of community-spirited progress. These kids were the proud creation of postwar optimism, Dr. Spock rationalism, and Father Knows Best family order. Coming of age, however, Boomers loudly proclaimed their antipathy to the secular blueprints of their parents; they demanded inner visions over outer, self-perfection over thing-making or team-playing. The Boom "Awakening" climaxed with Vietnam War protests, the 1967 "summer of love," inner-city riots, the first Earth Day, and Kent State. In the aftermath, Boomers appointed themselves arbiter of the nation's values and crowded into such "culture careers" as teaching, religion, journalism, marketing and the arts. During the '90s, they trumpeted values, touted a "politics of meaning" and waged scorched-earth culture wars. *Bill Bennett, Hillary Rodham Clinton, John Ashcroft, Oprah Winfrey, Bill Gates, Laura Schlessinger, Rush Limbaugh, Spike Lee, Camille Paglia, Steven Spielberg.*

**Generation X** (Born 1961–81) survived a hurried childhood of divorce, latchkeys, open classrooms, and devil child movies. They came of age curtailing the earlier rise in youth crime and fall in test scores—yet heard themselves denounced as so wild and stupid as to put The Nation At Risk. As young adults, navigating a sexual battlescape of AIDS and blighted courtship rituals, they dated and married cautiously. In jobs, they embraced risk and prefer free agency over loyal corporatism. From grunge to hip-hop, their culture has revealed a hardened edge. Politically, they lean toward pragmatism and non-affiliation and would rather volunteer than vote. Widely criticized as "slackers," they triggered a positive turnaround in U.S. economic productivity yet still face a Reality Bites economy of pinched young-adult living standards. *Mark Andreessen, Michael Jordan, Cindy Crawford, Tom Cruise, Michael Dell, Jesse Jackson Jr., Winona Ryder, Quentin Tarantino, Laura Ingraham, Mike Tyson.*

**The Millennial Generation** (Born 1982–now) first arrived when "Baby on Board" signs appeared. As abortion and divorce rates ebbed, the popular culture began stigmatizing hands-off parental styles and recasting babies as special. Child abuse and child safety became hot topics, while books teaching virtues and values became best-sellers. By the mid-'90s, politicians were defining adult issues (from tax cuts to PBS funding to Internet access) in terms of their effects on children, Hollywood replaced cinematic child devils with child angels; cable TV and the Internet cordoned off child-friendly havens. While educators spoke of standards, cooperative learning, and school uniforms, community service surged in popularity. In the late '90s, the media spotlight—and focus of political debate—shifted to high school students. After the high school class of 2000 entered college, the media began featuring stories about new collegians, along with "good news" stories about how teens were turning against risk. *Taylor and Zac Hanson, Ashley and Mary-Kate Olsen, Sarah Hughes, Frankie Muniz, Haley Joel Osment, Tara Lipinski, Megan Kanka, Amanda Bynes.*

Millennials arrived during the recent era of the "Culture Wars," while Gen Xers embarked on their young-adult dot-com entrepreneurialism.

America could now be entering a new post-9/11 era. How the "War on Terror" will affect Millennials over time, as they become young adults, is a matter of speculation. So far, the mood is reinforcing several Millennial traits and desires that were already apparent—including their orientation toward personal safety, family closeness, community action, applied high-tech, and long-term planning.

Millennials live in a world that has taken trends Boomers recall from their childhood and turned them upside down. Boomers can recall growing up with a homogenizing popular culture and wide gender-role gap in an era when community came first and family stability was strong (though starting to weaken). Millennials have grown up with a fragmenting pop culture and a narrow gender-role gap in an era when individuals came first and when family stability was weak (though starting to strengthen).

As a postwar generation, Boomers arrived just when conforming, uniting, and turning outward seemed the nation's logical priority. As a post-awakening generation, Millennials began to arrive just when diversifying, atomizing, and turning inward seemed preferable. Such reversals reflect a fundamental difference in the two generations' location in history.

Millennials also represent a sharp break from Generation X. Gen Xers can recall growing up as children during one of the most passionate eras of social dissent and cultural upheaval in American history, an era in which the needs of children were often over-looked or discounted. All this has left a deep impression on most of today's young Gen X adults.

But Millennials can recall none of it. They have no personal memory of the ordered Cold War world (when only large and powerful governments had weapons of mass destruction). They only know about a post-Cold War era of multilateral confusion and power vacuums (when terrorists and rogue states are seeking these weapons). This generation has been shaped by such formative collective experiences as Waco, Oklahoma City, Columbine, the World Trade Center, and now 9/11 and the War on Terror. In all these instances, the real danger seems to come not from out-of-control institutions, but from out-of-control individuals, or small groups of conspirators, who have become a menace to humanity because national or global institutions are not strong enough to even monitor them.

How Boomers and Gen Xers have responded to their own location in history is a story that is mostly written, a story replete with ironies and paradoxes. How Millennials will respond to theirs is a drama waiting to unfold. Yet if you know what to look for and why, certain themes in this drama can be anticipated, and their implications become clear.

## How Every Generation Rebels

If it's true (as Alexis de Tocqueville once wrote) that "in America, each generation is a new people," does some pattern or dynamic help us determine how each generation will be new?

Yes.

Three basic rules apply to any rising generation in nontraditional societies, like America, that allow young people some freedom to redefine what it means to be young, and to direct society according to their own inclinations—in other words, to "rebel."

First, each rising generation breaks with the young-adult generation, whose style no longer functions well in the new era.

Second, it corrects for what it perceives as the excesses of the current midlife generation—their parents and leaders—sometimes as a protest, other times with the support of parents and leaders who seek to complement their own deficiencies.

Third, it fills the social role being vacated by the departing elder generation.

When you apply these rules to the generational dynamic in America, you can see what's been happening, and will continue to happen even more powerfully, with Millennials.

Stylistically, today's teens are breaking with today's thirtyish Gen Xers and the whole "X" (and "X-treme") attitude. Expect teamwork instead of free agents, political action instead of apathy, technology to elevate the community and not the individual, T-shirts with school colors instead of corporate swooshes, on-your-side teamwork in place of in-your-face sass.

Gen Xers in their late twenties and thirties often regard themselves as the trend-setters of the teen culture, but often they know little about what actually goes on there. People that age are usually too old to have teens as siblings and too young to have teens as children. So they fall out of touch and, in time, a new batch of teens breaks with their culture. This happened in the early 1960s, again in the early 1980s, and it's starting to happen again.

Meanwhile, Millennials are beginning to correct for what teens see as the excesses of today's middle-aged Boomers: narcissism, impatience, iconoclasm, and a constant focus on talk (usually argument) over action. In their "rebellion," Millennials are starting to opt for the good of the group, patience, conformism, and a new focus on deeds over words. When they argue, it is less among themselves, and more with older generations whose members stand in the way of civic progress. With adults of all philosophical stripes yearning for "community," the Millennial solution is to set high standards, get organized, team up, and actually create a community. Unlike Boomers, Millennials won't need three days at a retreat to figure out how to rewrite a mission statement.

The third rule of rebellion may be the key to understanding not just what Millennials are now doing, but where they see their clearest path in the years ahead.

Remember those whom Tom Brokaw christened the "greatest generation"—the ones who pulled America out of Depression, conquered half the globe as soldiers, unleashed nuclear power, founded suburbia, and took mankind to the moon. The most important link this "G.I. Generation" has to today's teens is in the void they leave behind: No other adult peer group possesses anything close to their upbeat, high-achieving, team-playing, and civic-minded reputation. Sensing this social role unfilled, today's adults have been teaching these (G.I.) values to Millennials, who now sense the G.I. "archetype" as the only available script for correcting or complementing the Boomer persona.

Today's Millennial teens often identify the G.I.s as their grandparents. When asked in surveys to assess the reputations of older generations,

Millennials say they have a much higher opinion of G.I.s and a somewhat lower one of Gen Xers than they do of any generation in-between—Boomers (the children of the postwar American High) or the Silent (the children of

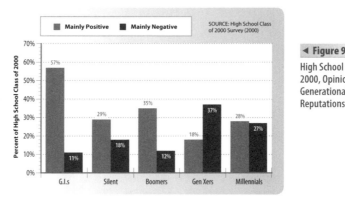

World War II). Many speak glowingly about G.I.s as men and women who "did great things" and "brought us together as a nation."

In a 2001 *Atlantic Monthly* cover story, author David Brooks has labeled Millennials "Organization Kids," a tacit reference to the original G.I. "Organization Man," and about as far as you can get from the "Bourgeois Bohemians" Brooks finds so common among the middle-aged.

Teens in 2001 don't rebel against midlife Boomers by being hyper-Xers—not when the oldest Xers are themselves entering the fortysomething bracket. They rebel by being G.I. redux, a youthful update of the generation against which the Boomers fought 30 years ago. No one under the age of 70 has any direct memory of teens, or twentysomethings, who resemble G.I. in spirit.

Millennials embody that spirit. That's why what's around the corner looks to be so profound that it might better be called a youth revolution. Rebellions peter out—but revolutions produce long-term social change.

# 3 | Life Before College

"We like to let people in on a little secret. These kids are less likely to take drugs, less likely to assault somebody else, less likely to get pregnant, and more likely to believe in God."

— VINCENT SHIRALDI, JUSTICE POLICY INSTITUTE (2000)

# Life Before College

Let's walk through the recent history of American childhood—an era that seems like only yesterday:

The February 22, 1982 issue of *Time* offers a cover story about an array of thirtysomething Boomers choosing (finally) to become moms and dads. This same year, bright yellow "Baby on Board" signs begin popping up in station-wagon windows.

Around the 1983 Christmas time, adult America falls in love with Cabbage Patch Kids—a precious new doll, harvested pure from nature, so wrinkly and cuddly-cute that millions of Boomers want to take one home to love. Better yet, why not a genuine, live Millennial?

*The era of the wanted child had begun.*

In September 1982, the first Tylenol scare leads to parental panic over trick-or-treating. Halloween suddenly finds itself encased in hotlines, advisories, and statutes—a fate that will soon befall many other once-innocent child pastimes, from bicycle-riding to BB guns.

A few months later comes national hysteria over the sexual abuse of toddlers, leading to dozens of adult convictions after what skeptics will liken to Salem-style trials.

All the while, new books (*The Disappearance of Childhood, Children Without Childhood, Our Endangered Children*) assail the "anything goes" parental treatment of children since the mid-1960s. Those days are ending; the family, school, and neighborhood wagons are circling.

*The era of the protected child had begun.*

The early 1980s are when the national rates for many behaviors damaging to children—divorce, abortion, violent crime, alcohol-intake, and drug-abuse—reach their postwar high-water mark. The well-being of children begins to dominate the national debate over most family issues: welfare, latchkey households, drugs, pornography.

In 1983, the federal *Nation at Risk* report on education blasts grade-school students as "a rising tide of mediocrity," editorialists implore teachers and adults to do better by America's next batch of kids.

In 1984, "Children of the Corn" and "Firestarter" bomb at the box office. Hollywood is astonished, since these are merely the latest installments in a child-horror film genre that has been popular and profitable for well over a decade, ever since "Rosemary's Baby" and "The Exorcist." But parents suddenly don't want to see them. Instead, they begin flocking to a new kind of movie ("Baby Boom," "Parenthood," "Three Men and a Baby") about adorable babies, wonderful tykes, and adults who improve their lives by looking after them.

*The era of the worthy child had begun.*

In 1990, the *Wall Street Journal* headline—"The '60s Generation, Once High on Drugs, Warns Its Children"—is echoed by The *New York Times*: "Do As I Say, Not As I Did." Polls show that Boomer parents do not want their own children to have the same freedom with drugs, alcohol, and sex that they once enjoyed.

By the early '90s, elementary-school kids are in the spotlight. During the Gulf War Super Bowl of 1991, children march onto the field at halftime amid abundant media coverage. By the early '90s, elementary-school kids are in the spotlight. During the Gulf War Super Bowl of 1991, kids march onto the field at halftime amid abundant media coverage (unseen during the Vietnam War) of the children of dads serving abroad.

# What Millennials Don't Remember

At Beloit college, Professor Tom McBride and his colleagues have drawn up a list of the major ways the Millennial experience of society has differed from that of older Americans. He says: "We assemble this list out of a genuine concern for our first-year students, and as a reminder to the faculty of the gap that may exist between generations. Education is the best remedy for the situation, but we start out with varying points of reference and cultural touchstones." Among the highlights, for members of the class of 2004:

..................................................................................................

1. Most students entering college this fall, in the class of 2004, were born in 1982.
2. Grace Kelly, Elvis Presley, Karen Carpenter, and the E.R.A. have always been dead.
3. Kurt Cobain's death was the "day the music died."
4. Somebody named George Bush has been on every national ticket, except one, since they were born.
5. The Kennedy tragedy was a plane crash, not an assassination.
6. Huckleberry Finn has always been a "banned book."
7. A "45" is a gun, not a record with a large hole in the center.
8. They have no clue what the Beach Boys were talking about when they sang about a 409 and a Little Deuce Coupe.
9. They have probably never lost anything in shag carpeting.
10. MASH and The Muppet Show have always been re-runs.
11. Punk Rock is an activist movement, not a musical form.
12. They have always bought telephones, rather than rent them from AT&T.
13. The year they were born, AIDS was found to have killed 164 people; finding a cure for the new disease was designated a "top priority" for government-sponsored research.
14. We have always been able to reproduce DNA in the laboratory.
15. Wars begin and end quickly; peace-keeping missions go on forever.
16. There have always been ATM machines.
17. The President has always addressed the nation on the radio on Saturday.
18. We have always been able to receive television signals by direct broadcast satellite.
19. Cities have always been trying to ban the possession and sale of handguns.
20. Watergate is as relevant to their lives as the Teapot Dome scandal.
21. They have no idea that a "presidential scandal" once meant nothing more than Ronald Reagan taking President Carter's briefing book in "Debategate."
22. They have never referred to Russia and China as "the Reds."
23. Toyotas and Hondas have always been made in the United States.
24. There has always been a national holiday honoring Martin Luther King, Jr.
25. Three Mile Island is ancient history, and nuclear accidents happen in other countries.
26. Around-the-clock coverage of Congress, public affairs, weather reports, and rock videos have always been available on cable.
27. Senator Phil Gramm has always been a Republican.
28. Women sailors have always been stationed on U.S. Navy ships.
29. The year they were born, the *New York Times* announced that the "boom in video games," a fad, had come to an end.
30. Congress has been questioning computer intrusion into individuals' personal lives since they were born.
31. Bear Bryant has never coached at Alabama.
32. They have always been able to afford Calvin Klein.
33. Coors Beer has always been sold east of the Mississippi, eliminating the need for Burt Reynolds to outrun the authorities in the *Smokey and the Bandit* films.
34. They were born the same year that Ebony and Ivory lived in perfect harmony.
35. The year they were born, Dustin Hoffman wore a dress and Julie Andrews wore a tuxedo.
36. Elton John has only been heard on easy listening stations.
37. Woodstock is a bird or a reunion, not a cultural touchstone.
38. They have never heard a phone "ring."
39. They have never dressed up for a plane flight.
40. Hurricanes have always had men's and women's names.
41. Lawn darts have always been illegal.
42. "Coming out" parties celebrate more than debutantes.
43. They only know Madonna singing American Pie.
44. They neither know who Billy Joe was, nor wondered what he was doing on the Tallahatchee Bridge.
45. They never thought of Jane Fonda as "Hanoi Jane," nor associated her with any revolution other than the "Fitness Revolution" videotape they may have found in the attic.
46. The Osmonds are talk show hosts.
47. They have never used a bottle of "White Out."
48. If they vaguely remember the night the Berlin Wall fell, they are probably not sure why it was up in the first place.
49. "Spam" and "cookies" are not necessarily foods.
50. They feel more danger from having sex and being in school than from possible nuclear war.

Between 1986 and '91, the number of periodicals offered to young children doubles, and between 1991 and '94, the sale of children's music also doubles. In tot-TV fare, "Barney and Friends" (featuring teamwork and what kids share in common) steals the limelight from Sesame Street (featuring individualism and what makes each kid unique).

During 1996, major-party nominees Dole and Clinton duel for the presidency in a campaign with plenty of talk about the middle-school children of "soccer moms."

During 1997, Millennials begin to make an impression on the pop culture. Thanks to the Spice Girls, Hanson, and others, a whole new musical sound appears—happier, brighter, more innocent. "They like brands with heritage. Contrived, hard-edged fashion is dead. Attitude is over," MTV president Judy McGrath says of her company's new teen interns. "They like what's nice and fun in fashion and sports. They like the Baby Gap ads; they're simple and sweet."

*The era of the perfected child had begun.*

Actually, those MTV interns were late Xers, born a little before 1980. But the big change—the revolution in youth—is coming from those 1982-86 birth cohorts. Other key trends await the Millennials' second wave, born later in the 1980s. Test scores, though improving gradually for first-wavers, are likely to ramp up steeply once today's heavily homeworked, super-tested tweens enter high school. By the time the preteens of 2001 reach college age, and campuses are a hotbed of Millennial styles, the true Millennial persona will reveal itself in full force.

Boomers started out as the objects of loosening child standards in an era of conformist adults. Millennials have started out as the objects of tightening child standards in an era of nonconformist adults. By the time the last Millennials come of age, they could become the best-educated youths in American history, and the best-behaved young adults in living memory. But they may also have a tendency toward copying, consensus, and conformity that educators will want to challenge, as well as many other character traits that will require broad changes in the academy.

Through the late 1990s, these same much-watched children passed through high school, accompanied by enormous parental, educational, and media fascination—and headlines, not all of them positive. After the April 1999 Columbine tragedy was replayed again and again on the news, this adult absorption with Millennial safety, achievement, and morality reached a fever pitch.

Eighteen months after Columbine, these wanted, protected, worthy, perfected children began entering college.

Twenty years ago, the arrival of Generation X on campus took many institutions of higher learning by surprise. Professors and administrators began noticing that incoming students were less interested in the protest movements that had driven college life throughout the 60s and 70s. The level of intellectual engagement seemed to drop precipitously. Students no longer debated professors about the curriculum. Why bother with what anyone else thinks, when you can simply vote with your feet, switch classes, and stick with your own niche?

The Gen X attitude toward knowledge was more instrumental. In history classes, students were less likely to ask about which wars were moral than about how you win one. Many of the highly motivated students gathered in professional schools, where the object was less to change the world than to make a lot of money. A good student was one who could get the best transcript with least possible expenditure of effort—a bottom-line focus which Gen Xers maintained as entry-level workers in the late '80s and '90s, with wondrous consequences for the economy's productivity.

Think about all of the ways that institutions of higher learning had to adjust to fit this style of student. *In loco parentis*, already under assault during the 60s and 70s, virtually disappeared. Pass/fail grading options became available for many if not most classes, and core curricula requirements relaxed. Widespread use of drug and alcohol forced colleges and universities to build new relationships with local police. Speech codes were enacted to counter uncivil discourse. Large, school-wide events became less common, as cynicism about school spirit and campus community spread. Students took longer to earn their degrees.

The college clientele changed in the Gen X era, as well. More foreign, older, and "continuing education" students were enrolled. To meet shifting demand, driven by changing economic conditions, business and law schools expanded, while science and engineering departments were increasingly the province of international students.

Now, with the arrival of the Millennials, campus life is due for another transformation. Policies needed to accommodate or manage college students in the '80s and '90s will become increasingly inappropriate. Instead, professors and administrators will have to adjust their institutions to a new crop of students who will be:

* Close with their parents.
* Extremely focused on grades and performance.
* Very busy in extracurricular activities.
* Eager for community activities.
* Talented in technology.
* More interested in math and science, and less interested in the humanities.
* Demanding of a secure, regulated environment.
* Respectful of norms and institutions.
* Conventionally minded, verging on conformist thinking.
* Ethnically diverse, but less interested than their elders in questions of racial identity.
* Majority female, but less interested than their elders in questions of gender identity.

They also are very numerous, and very intent on going to college, which will make these trends all the more consequential.

# 4 | Millennials
# By the Numbers

"It's great! Nobody is plain white, or plain black, or plain anything. Eventually I'm hoping every place will be like this."

— LIZ SHORT, TEENAGER AT A MIXED-RACE SYMPOSIUM AT WELLESLEY COLLEGE (2000) —

# Millennials By the Numbers

To demographers and economists, each new generation brings with it a new batch of numbers and trend lines. One good test of whether we can draw an accurate qualitative profile of a generation is whether this profile matches the numbers. Let's take a new look at Millennials by the numbers: their size, their diversity, the dollars they spend, and the hours they work.

## The Baby Boomlet

The best-known single fact about the Millennial Generation is that it's large. Already, America has well over 80 million Millennials. By the time future immigrants join their u.s.-born peers, this generation will probably top 100 million members, making it nearly a third bigger than the Boomers. In native births per birth year (expected to average 3.9 million), Millennials will tower over Gen Xers, Boomers, and every earlier generation in America.

Since most Millennials born in the 1980s are the children of Baby Boomers, the media often refers to them as America's new "Baby Boomlet"

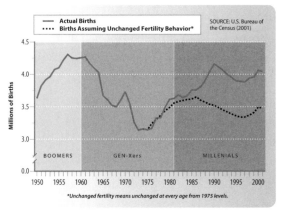

**◄ Figure 10**

Total U.S. Births, in Millions, 1950 to 2001

or "Echo Boom" generation. In two key senses, these terms are misleading. First, the 1990s-born Millennials—the larger half of the generation—are primarily the children of Gen Xers, not Boomers. And, second, these terms imply that the large number of Millennials is mainly a matter of arithmetic, as though a "baby boomlet" mechanically had to issue from "baby boom" parents. Not so. Most of the boomlet reflects higher fertility—the greater likelihood by the mid-'80s over the mid-'70s that the typical woman of childbearing age will have a baby. For the most part, what gave rise to the large number of Millennials was the desire of their parents to bear and raise more of them.

The large size of this generation is primarily an extension of the early-'80s shift in adult attitudes toward children that greeted their first-born members. The arrival of Generation X in the early '60s coincided with an era of decline in the u.s. fertility rate and a society-wide aversion to children. And so it remained for the following 20 years, as small children seldom received positive media, and adults complained to pollsters about how family duties hindered their self-discovery. Children became linked to new adjectives: unwanted, at-risk, throwaway, homeless, latchkey.

By 1975, when annual births had plunged to barely three million—versus over four million in the late 1950s—newspapers talked about Gen Xers as America's new "Baby Bust" generation. Baby-market companies, like Gerber Products, were hit hard. Starting in 1977, annual births tilted back up again, slowly at first, and the baby industry began bouncing back. By the early 1980s, Gerber and the others were rescued by a floodtide of new babies, who also brought good cheer to the manufacturers of cribs, strollers, rockers, safety seats, PJs, dolls, safety gadgets, and toddler books and videos.

Most experts contended that the late-'70s birth surge would be short-lived, but they were in for a surprise. After leveling off at about 3.6 million during 1980–83, the national birth rate did not drift back down. Instead, it rose-to 3.8 million in 1987, 4.0 million in 1989, and 4.2 million in 1990. In many regions, hospital delivery rooms became overcrowded and pediatricians hard to find. During the 1990s, the annual number of births again drifted below the 4.0 million benchmark, until 2000 produced another surge in the fertility of young (this time, Gen X) women. Overall, Millennial births have been roughly 20 percent higher than if the fertility of women at each age had remained steady at mid-'70s rates.

During the 1960s and '70s, the era of Gen X babies, adults went to great efforts not to produce children, driving up demand for contraceptive technologies and for sterilization and abortion clinics. By contrast, during the Millennial baby era, adults have gone to great efforts to conceive and adopt babies. Sterilization rates, which rose sharply in the 1960s and '70s, plateaued in the middle '80s and have since fallen. The annual abortion rate, after ramping up during the Gen X baby era, hit a peak in 1980 and has since declined (through 1996) by 22 percent. Meanwhile, the share of all births declared to be "unwanted" by their mothers has also declined—with an especially sharp drop in unwantedness by African-American mothers.

What's important about the "baby boomlet" is how sustained it has been, and how it has reflected a resurgent adult desire to have kids. As a share of the population, America actually had more grade-school children during the tail-end years of the postwar "baby boom" than it does today. But back when those last Boomers were in elementary school, around 1970, the number of schoolchildren was trending downward—and steadily fewer adults wanted to bear them, make films or TV shows for them, or pay much public attention to them.

The 1990 peak of the Millennial birth bulge is now rippling up the age ladder and, in time, will hit the college age bracket. It already hit first-graders in 1997 and "tweens" in 2002. It will hit high school seniors in 2008, college seniors in 2012.

## Colors of the World

Millennials are the most racially and ethnically diverse, and least Caucasian, generation in U.S. history. As of 2002, non-whites and Latinos accounted for 37 percent of the 20-or-under population, a share half-again higher than for the Boomer age brackets, and nearly three times higher than for today's seniors.

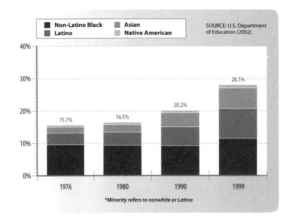

Figure 11 ▶
Minority* Share of
Total Students
Enrolled in U.S.
Institutions of
Higher Learning,
1976 to 1999

Ethnically, what differentiates Millennials from what Boomers recall of their own college years is the much vaster range of global diversity. The issue of color can no longer be defined in clear black-white (or even black-white-Latino) terms. A class full of Millennial collegians, even when one looks just at Americans, can include young women and men whose ancestors come from nearly every society on earth, including regions (Central and South America, subSaharan Africa, the Arab crescent, South Asia) that were far less represented on the campuses of the 1960s.

To this point, Millennials are less often immigrants themselves than the children of immigrants. One Millennial in five has at least one immigrant parent, and one in ten has at least one non-citizen parent. Containing more second-generation immigrants than any earlier twenty-year cohort group in U.S. history, Millennials embody the "browning" of American civilization. Thanks to the Internet, satellite news, porous national borders, and the Cold War's end, this is also becoming the world's first generation to grow up thinking of itself, from childhood forward, as global.

While Millennials are, indeed, a global generation, American (and Canadian) students mark the first leading edge, worldwide. Since World War II, the leading edges of new European generations have arrived two to five years after those in America. Euro-teens still resemble Gen X more than their American counterparts, but German youth experts are noting a Millennial-style shift now just reaching high school in that country. While generational patterns vary somewhat around the world, given each country's own particular history and culture, today's 20-year-old foreign student may in fact be part of a different generation than a 20-year-old American student. But that will be less true five years from now.

What about race? Does a generational dynamic that works for a generation's non-ethnic white majority also apply to its large non-white minority? Absolutely. In fact, non-white youths are often bigger contributors to this generation's emerging persona than white youths. Ask these questions: Which kids are most likely to be wearing school uniforms? Non-whites. Whose schools are moving fastest on back-to-basics drilling and achievement standards? Non-whites. Whose neighborhoods are producing the swiftest decline in street murder, child poverty, teen pregnancy, and school violence? Non-whites.

In fact, African-Americans have long been an outsized cultural contributor to generational currents, from civil rights (Silent Generation), to black power (Boomers), to hip-hop (Xers). That contribution continues, albeit in new forms, with today's urban schoolchildren far more likely than suburbanites to learn by rote and jointly shout upbeat slogans like, "I'm going to succeed!"

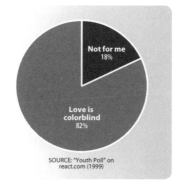

◀ Figure 12

Opinion on
Interracial Dating

Latino youths, now surpassing African-Americans in number, are powerful new ethnic contributors to American youth trends. With over half having at least one immigrant parent, many young Latinos face a future full of hard challenges: One-third live in poverty, in substandard housing, and without health insurance. The share of Latinos in grades 10–12 who drop out each year (9 percent) is much higher than for non-Latinos (5 percent). Problems are particularly acute for Latino boys, who have lower expectations for the future than their female counterparts. Yet many Latino pop icons provide a distinctly Millennial feel with upbeat lyrics, colorful clothes, dancing in couples, and close family ties. Asian teens are also a rapidly growing presence.

With parents even more attached to "family values" than the white adult majority, both the Latino and Asian youth cultures are setting a distinctly Millennial tone—positive, team-playing, and friendly—in schools and neighborhoods from Seattle to Boston, Miami to San Diego.

## Teens as a Target Market

Much of the interest in Millennials, as a generation, has been commercial—how to make them watch an ad, how to make them buy, how to use them to make their parents buy.

The reason for this is partly their sheer numbers, partly the affluence of the 1990s—but also a sudden awareness, among teen marketers, that generations matter. In the early 1990s, marketers awoke to the realization that they had never fully targeted Gen X, and they were determined not to let this mistake recur with the next batch of teens.

Today, no question, a lot more cash is being spent on young people than ever before, as anyone who has recently visited a typical teen bedroom can attest. Purchases by and for children age 4 to 12 tripled over the 1990s, and teens hit their stride at the decade's end. One youth marketing firm claims that more than $172 billion flowed through the hands of Americans aged 12 to 19 in 2001. By most accounts, that amount has dipped since 9/11, but financial analysts agree that the amount has risen enormously over the past decade.

In recent years, everyone is spending more on children and teenagers—youths themselves, parents on their own kids, and non-parents on their young friends and relatives. Adults are favoring this new generation by steering more money toward its wants and less toward their own, and by identifying its wants with their own. Many Americans worry that all this spending is spoiling young people who know no era other than a decade of affluence.

Plainly, not all teens have shared equally in the recent prosperity, nor in the child absorption that has come with it. Even so, child poverty rates in every racial and ethnic group have now reached record lows and, at the moneyed end of the spectrum, there's been a boom in pricey summer camps (for which weekly bills can top $2,000) and—at least until 9/11—ever-denser crowds at theme parks. You can see crowds of rich Manhattan teens with Prada handbags and designer clothes, yet also teens in poor neighborhoods with enough electronic gear to stock a small store. Major companies keep adding new product lines just for Millennials, such as Kids' Aquafresh, Pert Plus for Kids, Dial for Kids, even Ozark Spring Water for Kids.

## The Parent-Child Copurchase

Most of the Millennial spending boom is fueled by parental money, not their own. Over the past 15 years, the types of kid income rising the most are the types that parents most firmly manage (gifts, joint purchases, and paid household work). The types that have risen the least—or even declined—are the types parents least control ("allowances" and paid employment). Both trends defy the free-agent "proto-adult" youth stereotype of the Gen X youth era.

The fastest-growing source of teen cash has been the direct ad-hoc payment from parent to child, often for a specific purchase on which parent and child confer. Since such payments are neither child spending nor parent spending, these consensual transactions resist the categories favored by many marketing experts. One third of all teens now say ad-hoc cash from parents is their biggest source of income. Supplementing parental payments are gifts from grandparents, 55 percent of whom say they've given their grandkids one or more gifts in the prior month.

Another rapidly growing teen cash source is income earned through household chores, which often mingles with the parental "gift" category. In the Millennial child era, more parents are working longer hours. Millennials spend substantially more time than Gen Xers did on tasks previously performed by a parent, from food shopping to cooking to laundry to caring for siblings. And they're being paid for it. From 1991 to 1997, money from teen chores more than doubled.

Other income sources are falling in importance, including "allowances." To Boomer and Gen Xer parents, each dollar in "allowance money" seems wasted when that same dollar might to used to reward, instruct, punish, cajole, or moralize. Income from paid employment (outside the home) is also falling in importance.

As a consequence, teens are buying more things jointly with their parents. Teens ask parents for money to buy something, they together discuss whether it's a worthwhile purchase, the parents hand out the money, and teens go to the store (or on-line) to make the purchase. Officials at the Center for a New American Dream have noted a new "nag factor" driving many youth purchases, with 10 percent of 12- and 13-year-olds saying they ask their parents more than 50 times for products they've seen advertised.

While parents are often paying in full for major teen purchases (like cars, including insurance) that in times past were more financed by youth work and savings, parents appear to be influencing teen purchase decisions through rules, advice, and earmarked cash. At the same time, teens are influencing parental purchase decisions on big-ticket items like cars, houses, and vacations (by voicing their opinion) and on small-ticket items like groceries and take-out food (by saving their parents' time).

Thus has emerged the era of the parent-teen "copurchase."

Twenty years ago, the big new trend in youth marketing was the independent child purchase. Today, the big new trend is the child purchasing only after receiving a parent's approval, alias the "copurchase." When Nickelodeon set up shop in the early 1980s, it successfully promoted itself to Xer tweens as a "parent-free zone." A decade later, when the focus-group reaction was no longer favorable, Nick junked the slogan.

Teens frequently consult with parents on buying decisions. "Today's working parents feel so guilty about not spending time with their children that they try to compensate by offering them more consumer power," *The Financial Times* reported in 1997. "Others believe today's child-rearing practices fit in with Baby Boomers' respect for individual desires. And others say children's participation in purchasing decisions reflects, in part, parents' uncertainty about high-technology items." These days, more ads than ever before are "cross-over," aimed at parents and their teenage or younger children.

## Organization Kids

For Millennials, job time, job experience, and job income, are all shrinking aspects of teen life.

Year to year, teen employment usually tracks the patterns of adult employment. In a recession, when one peaks, the other typically does so at about the same time. Yet over the longer term, teen employment shows little relation to the employment of older age brackets. For example, you would think the stagflationary '70s would have been a shakeout time for teen workers, and the roaring '90s a growth time, but very much the opposite occurred.

From one generation to the next, shifting parental and youth attitudes have played key roles in pushing teen employment up or down. It was low for the Silent, rising for Boomers, and high for Gen Xers—and now, for Millennials, falling again.

For Boomer teens, the "right" to work was a newly won youth freedom. Then Gen Xers came along and pushed teen workloads higher. Summer and after-school teen work grew strongly and almost continuously from the mid-'60s to the early '80s, when late-wave Boomers and first-wave Xers (girls especially) pushed paid teen employment to an unprecedented peak. Xers kept it near these high levels for the rest of the decade.

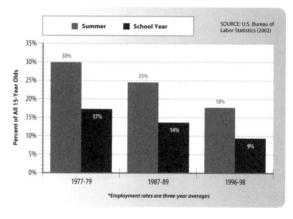

◄ **Figure 13**

Employment Rate of
15-Year-Olds, Late '70s
to Late '90s

Throughout the Gen X youth era, the purpose of teen work was shifting away from supporting families and toward personal spending money, career-building, or self-fulfillment. One of every six 15-year-olds held an after-school job, one of every three a paid summer job, and, for the first time ever, employed girls outnumbered employed boys. Later in the 1980s, as adult immigrants began moving into the service sector, teen employment began to ebb slightly. By the late '80s, employment rates for 16- and 17-year-olds were roughly 5 percent below those of the late '70s. Rates for 15-year-olds were 20 percent lower.

In the Millennial youth era, employment has continued to fall among teens, especially younger teens, despite an economy that (until recently) wanted workers and was willing to pay for them. By early 2002, the number of teenage girls working or looking for work had declined to 46 percent, the lowest since 1994. The percent of male teens in the labor market in 2002 was also 46 percent—the lowest ever recorded since record keeping began in 1948, according to the U.S. Bureau of Labor Statistics.

What accounts for the ebbing popularity of paid work for teenagers? Changing attitudes among teens and adults. During the 1990s, parents and educators began to have second thoughts about whether too many teens might be wrapping tacos when they should be wrestling with math. And more teens themselves now question whether unskilled work is a good use of time. When the bottom line is getting into college (especially when a family has the means to pay for it), time spent on computer lessons, select soccer, community service, or SAT prep courses seems more valuable, long-term, than nearly any kind of job.

This does not mean that Millennials are averse to gainful employment. To the contrary: Millennials like to plan, are focused on the future, and believe any work they do today should be a planned and preparatory investment for the permanent kind of life they wish to lead tomorrow. Compared to Gen X, they are more likely to find summer jobs that serve the community or teach new professional skills—and less likely to bother with jobs that simply generate spending money. The new popularity of the word "internship" is suggestive. Semester or summer, private or public, paid or unpaid, the jobs that today's collegians find most attractive are apprenticeships that promise to pay off over a lifetime.

## Big Brands Are Back

In teen purchasing power and youth market trends, a new generational universe is emerging. Millennials are beginning to reconnect the youth and adult markets, to reverse the inflow of school-age youths into paying jobs, and to reunite the splintered and narrowcast buying habits inherited from Gen X. They are transforming the commercial role of youth through positive peer pressure, cooperative choice-making with parents, and easily accessible new teen media. With e-stores, chat rooms, and buddy lists, they are the first youth generation in which virtually any member can keep up hour-to-hour with the opinions and tastes of peers across the nation.

Niche markets are endangered, and big brands are back. Aided by new technologies, from web chat to cell phones, Millennials pay keen attention to what's happening at the gravitational center of their peer group, whether on line at Delia's or alloy.com or in person at Target and Wal-Mart (both of which have enjoyed huge post-9/11 boosts in teen buying). Mass fads, group focus, and a lower-profile commercial style are ready for a come-back. Meanwhile, "the edge" has peaked—"In your face" campaigns, like Abercrombie & Fitch's recent ultra-edgy approach, are running into new resistance. And the day appears to have passed for weak product loyalties, hyper-commercialism, and the focus on risk and niche and self.

Many mass marketers have taken note of this. In the April 1998 issue of *American Demographics*, Texas A&M professor James McNeal explained how "Advertising that encourages children to defy their parents, make fun of authority, or talk unintelligibly will be replaced with informative ads describing the benefits of products." That was five years ago, so you can now substitute the word "teenagers" for "children." By 2010, those for-merly "informed" children will populate campuses. Today's collegians are clearly trending in this direction.

Whatever you're selling, whether soap, cars, or colleges, the way to connect with Millennials is to brand your image, target the mainstream, wrap yourself around positive youth values, and make room for parents in your message.

## Busy Around the Clock

Millennial teens may be America's busiest people.

Long gone are the old days of Boomer kids being shooed outside to invent their own games—or of Gen Xer kids being left "home alone" with a "self-care" guide. For most of today's kids, such a hands-off nurturing style would be considered dangerous, even abusive.

The new reality is structure, planning, and supervision. From 1991 to 1998, according to University of Michigan researchers, eighth and tenth graders showed sharp reductions in their share of those who engage "every day" or "at least once a week" in such open-ended youth activities as going to movies, cruising in cars and motorcycles, or walking around shopping malls. Vast majorities of high-school seniors say they are more looked-after and have less free time than their older brothers and sisters at the same age. During the 1990s, the sale of student day-planners soared from one million to 50 million. As 10-year-old Stephanie Mazzamaro told *Time* magazine: "I don't have time to be a kid."

Among pre-school and elementary-school kids aged 3 to 12, comparisons of time diaries between 1981 and 1997 revealed a stunning 37 percent decline in the amount of "unstructured" free time, from 52 to 33 hours per week. Beyond Internet-use, just where is this time going?

✱ **School:** Up by 8.3 hours per week—it's the single most expanded child activity. More kids aged 4 and 5 (known in earlier generations as "pre-schoolers") are now in school. More grade schools have early morning classes, after-school programs, hobby groups, prayer clubs, "extra learning opportunity" programs, and summer school, which is now mandatory in many districts for kids who score low on certain tests and don't want to repeat a grade. Federal

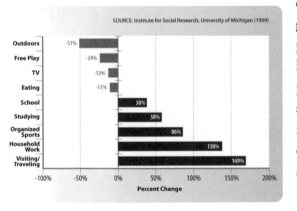

**Figure 14** ▶

Weekly Hours of Children Aged 3–12, by Activity Percent Change, 1981 to 1997

SOURCE: Institute for Social Research, University of Michigan (1999)

Outdoors -51%
Free Play -24%
TV -13%
Eating -11%
School 38%
Studying 58%
Organized Sports 86%
Household Work 138%
Visiting/ Traveling 169%

-100%   -50%   0%   50%   100%   150%   200%

**Percent Change**

spending on after-school programs is growing rapidly, even though 74 percent of elementary and middle-school parents say they would pay for such programs out of their own pocket, if necessary.

* **Household chores:** Up by 3.5 hours per week. Many more chores are done by today's kids, either alone or (as with grocery-shopping) with a parent.
* **Personal care:** (showering, hair care, dressing): Up by 3 hours. The let-it-be "nature child" of the Xer era is definitely passé.
* **Travel and visiting:** Up by 2.5 hours. This includes visits to non-custodial parents, who sometimes live in distant cities, or time spent in transit between scheduled events.

In short, today's rising generation is busy—and often not in ways that today's adults can recall from their own youth. Millennials are less likely to spend time lying on their backs imagining stories as they clouds roll by, and more likely to spend time learning how to excel at standardized tests. They are less likely to play self-invented games with made-up rules, ending when they feel like it, and more likely to play on select teams with adult referees, professionalized rules, and published standings.

Is this, in Gen X parlance, "a life"? Of course.

# 5 | Seven Core Traits

"Our generation isn't all about sex, drugs, and violence. It's about technology, discovery, and coming together as a nation."

— MIKAH GIFFIN, CJONLINE.COM (2000) —

# Seven Core Traits

Every generation is full of all kinds of people. But each generation has a persona, with core traits. Not all members of that generation will share those traits, and some may even personally rebel against them, but—like it or not—those core traits will define the world inhabited by every member of a generation.

Let's convert the data and trends into the following core traits. Over the next few years, evidence will mount that Millennials are:

* **Special**. From precious-baby movies of the mid-'80s to the media glare surrounding the high school Class of 2000, now in college, older generations have inculcated in Millennials the sense that they are, collectively, vital to the nation and to their parents' sense of purpose.
* **Sheltered**. From the surge in child-safety rules and devices to the post-Columbine lockdown of public schools, Millennials are the focus of the most sweeping youth-protection movement in American history.
* **Confident**. With high levels of trust and optimism—and a newly felt connection to parents and the future—Millennial teens are beginning to equate good news for themselves with good news for their country.
* **Team-oriented**. From Barney and soccer to school uniforms and group learning, Millennials are developing strong team instincts and tight peer bonds.
* **Conventional**. Taking pride in their improving behavior and quite comfortable with their parents' values, Millennials provide a modern

twist to the traditional belief that social rules and standards can make life easier.

* **Pressured**. Pushed to study hard, avoid personal risks, and take full advantage of the collective opportunities adults are offering them, Millennials feel a "trophy kid" pressure to excel.

* **Achieving**. With accountability and higher school standards rising to the very top of America's political agenda, Millennials are on track to becoming the smartest, best-educated generation in u.s. history.

On the whole, these are not traits one would have associated with Silent, Boomers, or Gen Xers, in youth, but they are traits remembered from the days of G.I. Generation teens.

## Millennials and Specialness

When today's political and business leaders create commissions and task forces, and undertake focus groups and surveys, their goal is often to find out more about youth issues. In 1998, more than half of all adults (a record share) said that "getting kids off to the right start" ought to be America's top priority. Even national issues having nothing directly to do with children—Social Security, war on terror, unemployment—are discussed in terms of their "child" impact.

As Millennials absorb the adult message that they dominate America's agenda, they come to the conclusion that *their* problems are the *nation's* problems, that *their* future is the *nation's* future, and that, by extension, the American people will be inclined to help them solve those problems.

Most Millennials are far more trusting than their parents of the capacity of large national institutions to do the right thing on their (and the nation's) behalf. When teens are asked who's going to improve the schools, clean up the environment, cut the crime rate, they respond—without irony—that it will be teachers, government, and police. In other words, they expect that people in those professions, hired by society to perform those critical social missions, should and will do their jobs.

Millennials are also more willing than other recent generations to acknowledge the importance of their own personal choices and actions. When asked about violence in schools, for example, the vast majority insist it's purely the fault of students—not of the culture, guns, or anything (or anyone) else.

When asked which groups will be most likely to help America toward a better future, teens rank "young people" ahead of government. When asked whose generation can have the greatest impact on what the global environment will become 25 years from now, 86 percent say their own, and only 9 percent say their parents'. When asked the same question, their parents mostly agreed, 71 percent saying their children's generation will have the most impact.

## Millennials and Sheltering

Throughout the '90s, Boomers and Gen Xers tightened the security perimeters around Millennials. Worried parents became avid consumers for a child-proofing industry that snapped up new patents for everything from stove-knob covers to safety mirrors. As voters, those same parents triggered a crusade for programs and policies to look after their children. The sheltering trend went in the reverse direction from what today's older generations recall from their own youth eras, when adult protectiveness was being dismantled (for Boomers) or was just plain weak (for Gen Xers).

For Millennials, the edifice of parental care has been like a castle that keeps getting new bricks added—V-chips and "smart lockers" last month, carding at the movies this month, graduated licenses and bedroom spy-cams next month. The older ones recall the most open sky, while the younger ones look up at the growing walls, unable to imagine what could be seen in their absence.

Younger Millennials, the ones still in elementary and middle school, appear to be even more supportive of extra protection than older ones in high school or college. A few months after Columbine, older teens wanted to "increase" rather than "decrease" school security by a two-to-one margin, while younger teens said the same by a four-to-one margin. When sweeping new rules such as school uniforms or student identity cards are first proposed, the usual experience is initial student resistance, but only until those measures are put in place, after which many students change their minds and become supportive. And, by huge majorities, Millennial teens support harsh punishments (including expulsion) for those who misbehave.

One-quarter of Boomers say they expect their children or grandchildren to live with them at some point during retirement. Compare this to the attitudes of the Boomers' own parents, whose yearnings for escape and independence gave rise to exclusive senior communities like Sun City and Leisure World. For better or worse, today's working-age parents plan to hover over their children far into the future. Over the past quarter-century, the attitude of every age bracket toward multigenerational households has shifted in a huge and favorable direction. In 1973, only 33 percent of young adults felt it was a good idea for older people to share a home with grown children. Fifty-six percent felt it was a bad idea. By 1994, those proportions had reversed themselves—to 55 percent versus 28 percent, respectively.

True to the wishes of adult America, Millennials are protected, feel protected, and expect to be protected-even, some might say, overprotected.

## Millennials and Confidence

In May 1997, Canadian journalist Deborah Jones dubbed Millennials the "Sunshine Generation," recognizing that on both sides of the border, tweens and teens comprise today's happiest age bracket. Where polls show adults believing that being a parent is getting harder, they show Millennials believing that being a kid is getting easier. Among teens, this is a very recent development. As late as 1994, 70 percent of (Gen X) 13- to 17-year-olds said it's "harder" to grow up now than in their parents' time. By 1999, among Millennials, that percentage had dropped to 43 percent.

"Why are kids so confident?" asks a recent KidsPeace report. "Significantly, the word 'crisis' seems not to appear in the teen lexicon." The Cold War is over. And even if the economy is slowing and the NASDAQ has a bad year, the Internet keeps getting faster and cell phones cheaper.

More than half of all teens agree that "people my age should be optimistic about their chances of having a good job." Among those in families earning less than $30,000, 54 percent believe the world holds "many opportunities for me." Among those in families earning over $75,000, that proportion rises to 78 percent. More than four in five teens (including 95 percent of Latinos and 97 percent of African-Americans) believe they will be financially more successful than their parents—a percentage that rose sharply during the 1990s.

The teen view of success has become better-rounded and less exclusively focused on one life goal. Over the last decade, "marriage/family" and "career success" have each declined in importance as "the one thing" in life. What's now more important is the concept of *balance*—between work and play, academic life and social life, and, down the road, between work life and family life. A rising share of high school seniors say "making a contribution to society" is "extremely" or "quite" important, while a declining share (though still a majority) say the same for "having lots of money."

In a turnabout from Gen X teens of the 1980s, Millennial teens have faith that the American Dream will work not only for them but for their own children. They see the future with a far longer view than their parents did, at the same age. The share of teens who define success as "being able to give my children better opportunities than I had" has reached an all-time high.

| Table 1: Freshman Attitudes, Then and Now | 1974 | 1983 | 1990 | 2001 |
|---|---|---|---|---|
| **Objectives considered essential or very important:** | | | | |
| Raising a family | 55% | 66% | 70% | 72% |
| Developing a meaningful philosophy of life | 61% | 44% | 43% | 43% |
| Being successful in my own business | 38% | 50% | 43% | 40% |
| **Agree strongly or somewhat:** | | | | |
| Marijuana should be legalized | 47% | 26% | 19% | 37% |
| Abortion should be legal | n/a | 55% | 65% | 55% |
| It is important to have laws prohibiting homosexual relationships | n/a | 49% | 44% | 25% |
| Sex is OK even if two people know little about each other | 46% | 49% | 51% | 42% |
| Realistically, an individual can do little to bring about changes in society | 44% | 37% | 31% | 26% |

n/a=not available
SOURCE: The American Freshman (UCLA, 1998–2001)

The events of 9/11 and the prospect of related economic shocks have shaken the confidence of many Millennials, but much less so than older Americans—yet, of all age groups, Millennials have proved to be the least perturbed by the new war rules, including violations of civil rights and intrusions against privacy. The reason: They already had their own 9/11, more than three years ago, in April of 1999, at Columbine High School in Littleton, Colorado. In the remaining six weeks of that traumatic school year, students learned what would happen if they kept a sharp object in their pocket, or played with a toy gun, or cracked a joke about student shooters; they had already been used to scanners, cameras, detectors, see-through backpacks, and unlockable lockers.

More than adults, Millennials have grown accustomed to the sight of SWAT teams and are more likely to associate such shows of force with safety. In this sense, teenage Millennials appear to be better prepared, functionally and emotionally, for the new mood of post-9/11 America.

## Millennials and Team-Orientation

Surrounded by individualistic older people, yet optimistic about their own abilities and prospects, Millennials have stepped into an Xer-styled teen world that, in their new view, had too little cohesion. They're now busy trying to make all the pieces fit together a bit better.

The team ethic shows up in a new youth aversion to disorder within their own social setting—starting with classrooms. When public school students are asked what most needs fixing in their schools, most of them mention teaching "good manners," "maintaining discipline in the classroom," and making students "treat each other with respect." Forty percent want something to be done about unruly student behavior that interferes with schoolwork.

Back in the Gen X youth era, educators disliked "peer pressure" because they associated the concept with rule-breaking. Today, educators are discovering that peer pressure can be harnessed—through student juries, peer grading, and the like—to enforce rules better.

The Millennials' team ethic shows up in their attitudes towards classmates. Honesty and hard work are now the highest-valued personal qualities, even though teens admit that those virtues do not necessarily lead to popularity. Ninety-five percent report that "it's important that people trust me." In choosing their peer leaders, Millennials say they look for maturity, friendliness, and quality of moral character ahead of an imaginative or independent mind.

The new teen belief in team play has broadened the search for peer friendships, drawing Millennials to circles and cliques. Only three teens in ten report that they usually socialize with only one or two friends, while two in three do so with groups of friends. The proportion of eighth- and tenth-graders who feel lonely or wish they had more friends declined sharply from 1991 to 1998. A rising share of today's collegians prefer to stay with their buddies after graduation (and, thanks to cell phones, many do). Teachers report that, compared with Gen Xers of a decade ago, today's students feel less close to teachers but closer to each other.

This Millennial cliquishness has made peer pressure a much more important teen issue than before, and they see more positive potential in it than adults normally do. Only about one-third of teens say they are under "a great deal" or "some" pressure from peers to "break rules," although a larger share report being teased about clothing, and bullying may be a rising problem.

Millennials are adapting new Internet, networking, and cell phone technologies to increase their level of interconnection. They're less interested in the anonymous freedom of the Internet and more interested in its potential to maintain their peer networks. Over 17 million U.S. teens were online in 2001, and seventy-five percent use Instant Messaging (IM) services. A typical Millennial can have one or two hundred "buddies" on her IM list. Isolated gaming is being replaced by multi-user "LAN parties," with Internet-wide gaming not far behind. And, of course, today's teens are driving the music industry into a steep recession with their web-based music sharing and CD burning.

This team ethic also shows up in the new political views of youth. When Millennial teens are asked to identify "the major causes" of America's problems, their seven most popular answers all pertain to what they perceive as an excess of adult individualism. Reason number one (given by 56 percent of all teens) is "selfishness, people not thinking of the rights of others." Reason number two (given by 52 percent) is "people who don't respect the law and the authorities." By contrast, "lack of parental discipline of children and teens"—an answer very few Boomer teens would ever have given—ranks as reason number four.

Millennials do see divisions, but not in the same places recalled by earlier generations. The Boomer rebellion of the 1960s was energized in the '70s by surging feminism—as gender became the greatest divide within their own generation. From the 1980s through the mid-'90s, rising immigration along with a new desire for self-help and a new tolerance of cultural fragmentation made race and ethnicity the greatest divide among Gen Xers. But now, among Millennials, gender, race, and ethnicity no longer carry the same voltage—but rising income inequality is making divisions of money and class an issue of rising youth concern. This will have major, long-term effects on entertainment, politics, culture—and campus life.

## Millennials and Convention

Boomer children felt overdosed on norms and rules, and came of age famously assaulting them. Millennials show signs of trying to re-establish a regime of rules. Where Boomer teens had trouble talking to their parents—a major cause of the late-'60s "generation gap"—Millennials have less trouble doing so. They favor moving to the center rather than explore the edge. It is not a conservative backlash, but a sense that rules and standards can sometimes make life easier.

Why this Millennial move to the center? Having benefited from a re-norming of family life following the turbulent 1960s and 1970s, today's teens are inclined to feel trust in the core aspects of their daily lives. Compared to Xers, Millennials bask in the sense of being loved by parents. In 1995, 93 percent of 10- to 13-year-olds felt "loved" all or almost all the time. In a 1997 Gallup survey, nine in ten youths reported being very close to their parents and personally happy—much closer than 20 years ago.

Millennials reveal a smaller "generation gap" with their parents than any teens in the history of polling. Two-thirds of today's teens say their parents are "in touch" with their lives, and six in 10 say it's "easy" to talk with parents about sex, drugs, and alcohol. In a 1998 teen survey, 80 percent reported having had "really important talks" with their parents, and 94 percent mostly or totally agreed that "I can always trust my parents to be there when I need them." (Back in 1974, more than 40 percent of Boomers flatly declared they'd "be better off not living with their parents.") Many parents report that their Millennial children tell them everything about their lives, far beyond what Boomers ever dared tell their own moms and dads.

Far more than anything Boomers can remember, today's teens and parents share tastes in clothes and music. Parents and children frequently agree on entertainment—-revivals of Boomer era music classics (e.g., Elvis) are sure-fire Millennial hits, and teens think nothing of introducing their parents to the latest Weezer album. What made "American Idol" so successful were all the families watching it together, parents and teens rooting together for shared favorites. Behind this trend lies a deeper agreement on underlying cultural values. The share of teens reporting "very different" values from their parents has fallen by roughly half since the 1970s; the share who say their values are "very or mostly similar" has hit an all-time high of 76 percent.

Yet if Millennials are broadly willing to accept their parents' values as stated, they are also starting to think they can apply these values, and someday run the show, a whole lot better. When asked whether "values and character" will matter more or less to their own generation when they're parents, they answer "more" by a two-to-one margin.

What this adds up to, is a generation of teens trying to reverse many of the dominant social and cultural trends of their childhood era. "One of the macro-trends we're seeing is neo-traditionalism," says teen-marketer Kirsty Doig. "These kids are fed up with the superficialities of life. They have not had a lot of stability in their lives. It's a backlash, a return to tradition and ritual." Millennials overwhelmingly favor the teaching of values in schools, including honesty, caring, moral courage, patriotism, democracy, and the Golden Rule.

Pollsters have recently expressed surprise at the new traditionalism (or at what some less accurately call the "new conservatism") of today's teens. As recently remarked by George Gallup, Jr.:

> *"Teens today are decidedly more traditional than their elders were, in both lifestyles and attitudes. Gallup Youth Survey data from the past 25 years reveal that teens today are far less likely than their parents were to use alcohol, tobacco and marijuana. In addition, they are less likely than their parents even today to approve of sex before marriage and having children out of wedlock. Teens want to reduce the amount of violence on TV; seek clear rules to live by, and promote the teaching of values in school. They are searching eagerly for religious and spiritual moorings in their lives. They want abstinence taught in school, and they think divorces should be harder to get.*

Researchers would not have said anything close to this about Boomers 40 years ago. On several of these topics, they would have said much the opposite.

## Millennials and Pressure

The new youth assumption that long-term success demands near-term achievement makes many Millennials feel extraordinarily pressured. What a high-school junior does this week determines where she'll be five and ten years from now. That, at least, is the new teen perception—and it's a reversal of a 40-year trend.

In their youth, Boomers felt *decreasing* pressure to achieve. Back when JFK-era hopes of a gleaming technocracy ran aground on Vietnam, youth riots, credibility gaps, and energy crises, Boomers perceived their future growing more chaotic, less linked to work or credentials, and less subject to institutional rules. A common youth view was that you could do almost anything you wanted in high school or (especially) college and not expect that your life would be all that affected by it.

Gen Xers inherited those trends and stepped into this mindset. While they were in school, the defining symptom of teen alienation was the widespread perception that success was often random, in a fast-moving, risk-rewarding economy that offered a lot more opportunities than guarantees to young people. To this mindset, long preparation was often a waste of time, and a quick move or stroke of luck was what often spelled the difference, good or bad.

For Millennials, the connection between effort and payoff is returning. Rather than breed a sense of entitlement, the buoyant economy has placed them into a pressure cooker. A rising population of well-credentialed high school seniors increases competition for the best college slots. Technology, with its constant demands for response to phone calls, email and instant messages, is putting additional demands on a teenager's time. Schools are passing out Day Timers, teachers are starting classes in "time management for kids," and parents are giving their teenagers Sean Covey's bestselling *The 7 Habits of Highly Effective Teens: The Ultimate Teenage Success Guide*.

The formula for youth today is: Success in life is the reward for effort plus planning. That's why many of today's "organization kids" feel stressed in ways that many of their parents never felt at the same age. It's also why the classic Xer doctrine—that a person can always rebound from failure—no longer seems as plausible. As Millennials apply to college with souped-up essays about so-called hardships, and testimonials about their hundreds of hours in community service, things like reputation and credentials matter more than ever before. Resume-building has become a stressful arms race. Constant pressure keeps Millennials moving, busy, purposeful—as a *New York Times* story from 2000 makes plain:

> *"For the first time this year, New York City…will use the results of the fourth-grade test to help determine whether children will be promoted to the next grade. Last year, 67 percent of New York City fourth-graders and 43 percent of fourth-graders in the rest of the state failed the*

*test." Sylvia Wertheimer, an assistant* D.A. *in Manhattan and mother of a fifth-grader, told the* Times *the new testing regime "really categorizes kids in the sense of a hierarchy, and kids are aware of it." Ms. Wertheimer went on: "[W]hat used to happen to us at the college level has now been brought down to fifth grade. The whole feeling is much more pressure, pressure, pressure."*

Grade inflation is continuing its three-decade-long trend. By 1998, one-third of all eighth graders, and one-fourth of all tenth graders, reported receiving an "A" or "A-" average. The impact of all those A's is simply to magnify the penalty of the occasional B or C—reinforcing the Millennials' fear of failure, their aversion to risk (and to out-of-the-box creativity), and their desire to fit in to the mainstream.

To many Millennial teens, it's as though they see a giant generational train ready to leave the station. Each of them believes they'll either be on the platform, on time and with their ticket punched, or they'll miss the train and never be on that platform again.

## Millennials and Achievement

Thirty years ago, many a Boomer had big plans. So does many a Millennial today. But that's where the similarity ends. Young Boomers often charted their future course by their own internal compasses, asking how a path felt rather than what it tangibly represented. Millennial teens are turning that around: They prefer timetables to compasses.

The majority of today's high-school students say they have detailed five- and ten-year plans for their future. Most have given serious thought to college financing, degrees, salaries, employment trends, and the like.

Millennials see these preparations as serious and important, but not exactly fun. The share of students who "try to do my best in school" keeps going up, but so does—among boys especially—the share who "don't like school very much" or "at all." All their lives, many Boomers have been driven to choose specialties and careers that in some way feel like personal vocations. Millennials would rather strike a balance between what they have to do and what they want to do, rather than merge the two (common among Boomers) or compartmentalize the two (common among Gen Xers).

In college, young Boomers made their biggest mark in the arts and humanities. As young professionals, they became precocious leaders in the media, teaching, advertising, religion—anything having to do with the creative rearrangement of values and symbols. Millennial teens show the opposite bent. Surveys reveal that they like math and science courses best, social studies and arts courses least—and like to spend free time in shared activities with friends, instead of doing imaginative, creative tasks on their own. Where young Boomers led stylistic rebellions in music, Millennials are waging a commercial rebellion. In theater, where young Boomers loved "improv," black costumes, and stripped-down sets, Millennials are reinventing Busby Berkeley choreography, elegant period costumes, and gorgeous sets.

Their collective ambitions also have a rationalist core. According to a LifeCourse Class of 2000 Survey, teens have a great deal of confidence in their generation's lifelong ability to improve technology (97 percent), race relations (77 percent), and the economy (55 percent)—all public and benchmarkable spheres of social life—but far less confidence in their prospects for improving more subjective areas such as the arts (31 percent), family life (20 percent), and religion (14 percent). Other surveys reveal teens as more likely than adults to value friendships, but less likely than adults to value the ability to communicate feelings.

# Part Two

Millennials are already the largest, most studious, and best-prepared pool of college applicants ever—and, in the years ahead, those trends will only broaden and deepen. Not only is their generation as huge as Boomers were, in youth, but an astounding 70 percent of its high school graduates plan to continue their education in some form after high school.

Where their Boomer parents as youths initiated an array of negative behavioral trends—in crime, suicide, accidents, substance abuse, sexual risk-taking—Millennials are pushing all those same trends in positive directions.

Yet with this good news come challenges. Millennials (and their parents) can be very demanding. They (and their parents) tend to be fixated on having only the "best" of this or that. They (and their parents) place enormous emphasis on the quality of campus life—from the strength of school spirit to the safety of dorms to the quality of mental health services and mentoring programs. They (and their parents) will consult and enlist "the team" if things don't go well.

While the rising demand for a college education will allow institutions of higher learning to become more choosy about which applicants they admit, the applicants (and their parents) are becoming more choosy about what they demand from higher education. Their list of "needs" could bankrupt even the wealthiest of universities. Among these is the "need" to find affordable tuition, to get offered a generous scholarship, to avoid crushing student loans—or, at the other edge, to avoid feeling like the only person in the dorm who is paying "full freight."

Meanwhile, many institutions will feel a real cost squeeze. At this writing, many private colleges are suffering major contractions in endowment assets and income, and many public schools are facing new budget cuts or tuition hikes mandated by legislatures in a time of flat or declining tax revenues.

Taken together—and when combined with the parental closeness and media glare that accompanies these young people wherever they go—all this translates into a very difficult set of choices for everyone from the smallest of colleges to the largest of megaversities. Unless the economy grows beyond what anyone can reasonably plan, no one will simply be able to "ride it out." Tough choices will have to be made.

What should a college do to cope with these new students—and to prepare for the onslaught of the even more Millennial-style classes to come? How should admissions, and campus life, and the classroom experience, be altered? Where should new money be spent? What should be done with tuition?

The seven core Millennial traits hold the key. For each of the seven, in turn, let's explore what the impact facing this new generation and the implications for the choices a college or university should make.

Some of these choices will be obvious, but others controversial. Rightly or wrongly, administrators and faculty members can be expected to resist a number of Millennial trends. That happens with every new generation. And perhaps it ought to happen, so long as universities strive to mentor according to timeless standards of character and professors strive to teach according to the timeless standards of their disciplines.

# 6 | Special

"In some ways they are as wholesome and devoid of cynicism as the generation that wore saddle shoes."

— NEW YORK TIMES (2000)

# Special

Quite unlike the Gen Xers who preceded them, today's Millennial collegians perceive that they're part of a special group of young people. Older generations have instilled in them the sense that they are collectively vital to the nation and individually vital to their parents' sense of purpose. For institutions of higher learning, this means that recruiting gifted students requires far more than just relying on reputation. It requires an explicit appeal to a sense of generational destiny (a strategy that would have rolled eyes of Gen Xers). And it requires making more effort to sell parents on the idea that your institution is precisely fitted to protect and educate their very "special" child.

## Implications for Recruiting and Admissions

This mutual perception of specialness, by college applicant *and* parents, explains why "copurchasing" is today so prevalent in the choice of college. Just as teens and parents jointly participate in the purchase of a son's clothes and a daughter's car (or a mom's computer), so too are parents and high schoolers jointly making college decisions.

Recruiting materials, and tours, should overtly acknowledge this trend. College brochures should show more adults than before, and should highlight features that may appeal less to students than to anxious parents—features like optimized "life plans" and close supervision and full-spectrum medical and counseling services, especially for "special needs" students with disabilities and diagnoses of various kinds.

A special child also wants to go to a special institution, where he or she will be prepared to play a special role. Stressing your institution's traditions, high standards, and involvement in national life is important for appealing both to Millennials themselves and to their parents. The new recruiting environment includes (a) Millennials who understand planning and have great expectations about adult-run institutions, in collaboration with (b) Boomer parents who, as they contemplate their advancing age, show ever greater willingness to position their own families in a long-term setting.

With young adults thinking long-term and parents talking "legacy," recruiting messages should become less personal and more historical. They should focus increasingly on a college's connection to history and to its institutional heritage. Recruiting materials should dare to be earnest in highlighting school history, student organizations, and ties to the local community. When there is a choice, Millennial specialness is best portrayed in collective images: photos of energized teams engaging in a campus-wide activity will work better than images of a lone enraptured scholar studying in the library or on the green.

### Implications for Campus Life

On freshman arrival day, college presidents give moms and dads the usual warm speeches about "up to now it's been your turn, now it's our turn." But today a new twist is required. Not only must institutions of higher learning pay more attention to parents in recruiting, they must also, like it or not, allow parents be more engaged in campus life. Many of today's parents have so much invested, emotionally and financially, in their children's well-being that they cannot quickly and entirely relinquish their role. This means that colleges and university must negotiate carefully with parents, manage their expectations, and understand that many of them may be experiencing their own rite of passage.

Wake Forest Dean Mary Gerardy describes a new social type affecting campus life, so-called "helicopter parents"—always hovering, ultra-protective, unwilling to let go, and enlisting what she calls "the team" (parent, physician, lawyer, other counselors) to assert a variety of special needs and interests.

The impact of "the team" will be particularly strong when dealing with "special needs" students. Given the large and rising number of grade school kids and tweens with various diagnoses, often specialized combinations of diagnoses, colleges can expect to see more of these students in the years ahead. Parents of these students have for years been accustomed to taking part in group decisions about every aspect of their child's life.

While their input may be instructive, Boomers will have more difficulty "letting go" than have other generations of parents. Many colleges are experimenting with new ways to handle this. Some are asking all parents and students to sign a "relationship covenant," which establishes what is and is not expected of all parties. Many schools are designing special parent programs for freshman orientation week, including "Parent Transition" seminars led by psychologists who help moms and dads work through the separation anxieties experienced by many of today's parents. At Seton Hall University in South Orange, N.J., following a formal orientation session in September of 2002, each of 600 parents was even given a teddy bear to stuff and dress in a T-shirt that read, "Somebody at SHU Loves Me."

Mom and dad can enjoy an ongoing taste of campus life through special newsletters, parent pages on college web sites, or targeted emails to parents of students known to be involved in certain activities. (Parents who for twelve years never missed their child's soccer game might enjoy an email telling how last week's contests turned out.) Colleges can craft and publicize special weekend occasions at which parents are welcome—and, when they visit, can provide rustic inns or conference centers to enable them to share more fully in the campus experience.

Think of the Boomers who today pursue "serious" vacations built around immersive experiences like dorming at a monastery, hiking through the jungle, or going into the barrio to erect housing. You can give them a similar "adventure travel" experience by enabling them to immerse themselves in the culture of your institution.

For many Boomer parents, a return to a campus environment can be, in some ways, the equivalent of their World War II-veteran parents' mid-life return to Normandy: an occasion to reminisce about what many will regard as most intense period of their lives, perhaps even the time they felt the most personally linked with broad historical currents. The challenge for a college is to enable Boomer parents to refresh this personal connection, without interfering with their own collegiate children's day-to-day experience.

Percent of Incoming Freshman Class with Parent Having at Least a College Degree, 1974–2001

On their own, Millennials will be enough of a challenge on campus life issues.

They have very high expectations for housing. Already, there's a new resistance to group bathrooms among a generation that, despite the recent Britney Spears bare-midriff fashion trend, is more physically modest than most older people might think. They are more inclined than prior collegians to want to undress only in private spaces. Group showers often go unused, even by athletes.

Millennials are more averse to having roommates than their Boomer parents were—in part because they are unfamiliar with that experience. One college survey found that three-quarters of incoming freshmen have never shared a room with anyone (even a sibling). That fact, combined with all the space-consuming tech gear students bring with them, makes the old classic dorm concept of two- (or three-) to-a-room feel archaic.

The most popular dorms are those featuring apartment-style clustering, with solo bedrooms wrapped around common areas, private bathrooms, and tiny kitchens. Off-campus housing—especially the large new "edge campus" apartment complexes springing up around major state universities—can give students more space and personal privacy, but offer less technology (broadband and cable hookups) and less sense of campus participation.

Millennials prefer meals to be available somewhere 24/7, or almost that. Even more than older Americans these days, today's collegians have largely lost the custom of formal sit-down meals and want to be able to munch whenever their harried schedules permit.

## Implications for the Classroom

At the personal level, specialness implies that every student be congratulated frequently for his or her progress through the curriculum. This requires progress to be carefully and regularly monitored, problems dealt with promptly or even preemptively, and no student allowed to fall by the wayside. The "no child left behind" approach that Millennials have experienced in grades K through 12 makes them expect that the difficulty of the subject matter will always be properly geared to each student's ability.

Before college, the education provided to "special needs" students has often been very individualized (and expensive). At colleges wishing to integrate these students into the general student body, administrators need to spell out precisely and in advance what types of teaching services and classroom adjustments will be made for them—and stick to those guidelines.

For all students, the key is feedback and structure. Constant quizzing and practice, regular instructor review, small projects, and an emphasis upon core skills mastery will be welcome. Large creative projects designed to "spread the class out" and one-time sink-or-swim exams will trigger anxiety, and perhaps resistance, from students and parents.

# 7 | Sheltered

"We have been hearing much of late about a return to the in loco parentis approach that fell out of favor in the late 1960s. The same baby boomers who fought to end these restrictions want to bring them back, perhaps out of dismay that their own children may have to make some of the same mistakes that they did."

—— JUDITH SHAPIRO, PRESIDENT OF BARNARD COLLEGE (2002)

# Sheltered

Everywhere Millennials go—from babyhood to childhood to adolescence and now to post-adolescence—they expect to be kept safe. College is no exception. Already, dormitories have tighter-than-ever security (in the Boomer days, they often had none), with many campuses converting to hotel-style keycards. On the one hand, parents will want their collegiate children to inhabit ivy-wrapped gothic buildings; on the other, they will worry about the healthfulness of what's inside, from water to ventilation. Some parents are buying houses near campuses for their collegiate children to live for four years, places where distant (and worried) parents can retain more control.

## Implications for Recruiting and Admissions

Campus security is now a sales point, and the lack of it is a real hindrance. To some degree, each college is a prisoner of its own geography, but no matter where a college may be located, it can take advantage of the state-of-the-art high-tech security many students and parents are now expecting. Accountability is key, and today's applicants (and parents) can scan the details for any college, including recent crime trends, at the federal Campus Security Statistics Website (http://ope.ed.gov/security/index.asp).

The Millennials' craving for safety—added to their close relationships with parents and now combined with recession and fear of terrorism—means that many colleges and universities can find new recruiting opportunities in their own back yards. A recent survey of college admissions officers by the National Association for College Admission Counseling indicates a rise in applications from in-state students, suggesting a growing reluctance to travel far from home.

Colleges that have always been safe (but have never really thought it very important) can now push this advantage explicitly in their marketing. One small college in Iowa that had long fielded a small plain-clothed security force put its officers in uniform to make "security" more conspicuously present to collegians and visiting parents.

As each year passes, any lapse of safety or security on a campus will bring far more media attention than before. Stories about campus crimes, suicides, accidents, or other tragedies will carry a graver risk that a college will suffer an enduring reputation loss than in the past, because of society's special concern for Millennials at whatever age they happen to be. The bonfire collapse that killed 12 Texas A&M students in 1999 was a one-day national story. A similar incident happening five years from now could well provoke Congressional investigations, mass forced resignations, and irrevocable damage to a school's reputation among prospective students and their parents.

The search for a "sheltered" environment may increase the appeal of small colleges. Many schools have long debated internally whether to be a "college" or a "university." For forty years, the fashion tide has been moving in favor of "university" and all that this word implies—a big, cosmopolitan, anonymous, professionalized place doing "world class" research. Many institutions formally changed their name, including the two dozen California "state colleges" that became "state universities" during the 1970s and 1980s. Starting with the Millennials, that tide is likely to shift. The idea of the "college" may lose its provincial stigma by projecting many of the virtues Boomer parents and their collegiate sons and daughters are seeking: a feeling of close community, small class size, teachers who care and know your name, *in loco parentis* rules, core curricula, traditions, and a shared enthusiasm for academics that transcends preparation for the professions.

Depending on the course of the War on Terrorism, the world could be a more dangerous (or, at least, uncertain) place for Millennial collegians than it was for Boomers or Gen Xers. Colleges with junior-year-abroad programs may need to enhance the security features of those programs. They may even want to relocate any that are in high-risk areas to reassure recruits and their parents about personal safety issues.

As events unfold, institutions that rely heavily on the recruitment and retention of foreign students may also face serious challenges. Immigration into the U.S. is likely to become more difficult, the visa rules more stringent, the official oversight more intrusive. Foreign students may be less inclined to come to the United States for college. Administrators would be wise to anticipate these changes by setting up proactive procedures—to prevent embarrassing problems at a time of great public anxiety; to reassure foreign students that, as long as they follow the rules, they can enroll without fear of official reprisal; and to preempt any complaints from American students and their parents.

## Implications for Campus Life

Today, in the eyes of many parents, students, political leaders, and the media, you cannot make a campus too safe. In the wake of 9/11, MIT increased its security budget by $1.5 million, money which bought, among other improvements, an armed guard at the university's reactor. According to a Sallie Mae questionnaire in January 2002, 47 percent of college and universities had significantly tightened security measures after the attacks. Whether or not such measures will continue to be warranted by the threat of terrorism, they play to preexisting Millennial-era interest in secure campus perimeters.

Safety concerns extend to misbehavior by students themselves. Student-on-student crime is declining, partly due to a declining rate of youth crime generally, but also because of no-nonsense college enforcement policies. More colleges and universities are freely sharing information with local law enforcement. Rowdy students at or after athletic games are facing new crackdowns. A less rambunctious style of Greek life may be emerging—

with tamer rushing and hazing, and more emphasis on upbeat extracurricular activities.

Contrary to public perception, teenage drinking has been falling for two decades. In 2002, the rate of alcohol use by incoming college freshmen hit a record low—partly because Millennials are less interested in casual boozing and partly because more colleges are offering alcohol-free dorms. Many campuses are using special stamps, bracelets, and cards to keep students into or out of certain dorms or buildings at certain hours, or to enforce alcohol age laws.

In recent years, cigarette smoking has remained at higher-than-desired levels among collegians, especially women, but here too change may be in the offing: The rate of teen smoking has fallen to the lowest level ever measured. Incoming freshmen will be familiar with zero-tolerance smoking rules (no smoking any time, any place) at their high schools. With them comes the opportunity for a college administration to establish new non-smoking rules and zones, which may be more controversial among campus employees and junior faculty than among the undergrads.

Polls reveal a mixed Millennial verdict on other forms of substance abuse—tolerance toward casual marijuana use, but a rising sentiment that students who do drugs are not popular. Surveys indicate that even at colleges where students aren't sure whether the actual use of alcohol and other drugs is declining, there is widespread agreement that such behavior is now less conspicuous and interferes less with normal student life. New abused substances (like ecstasy) may pop up from time to time, posing new discipline or health issues, but the overall trend should be toward fewer student problems in these areas.

Health services are a critical part of the whole safety equation. Since most Millennials have been raised by their parents to regard health care as a continuous process of monitoring and adjustment, colleges had better be staffed enough to handle frequent "wellness" checkups and the rapidly rising share of teens who require regular prescription medication. (In 2001 alone, annual national spending on prescription drugs for teens aged 18 and under rose by an astounding 28 percent.)

# FERPA
# and
# Boomer
# Parents

. . . . . . . . . . . . . . . . . . . . . . . . . . . . .

The Family Educational Rights and Privacy Act (FERPA) prohibits any school receiving federal funds (meaning just about any college) from releasing any part of the "educational record" of any student aged 18 or older to any outsider without the student's express permission. The "educational record" includes just about everything—grades, attendance, rule infractions, health records, and so on. To ensure this privacy, FERPA has required colleges to set up elaborate bureaucratic safeguards, along with special procedures by which students can access, amend, or appeal anything on file.

When FERPA was signed into federal law in 1974, the Watergate-stricken "Establishment" was reeling, and the reputation of Boomer collegians—who had just won the elimination of the military draft and a reduction in the voting age from 21 to 18—was riding high. The law's main original purpose was to keep government agencies like draft boards from prying into students' lives. The law also prevented parents from finding out what students were doing while at college. And while this was not FERPA's main purpose, most Americans believed this was fine. In the mid-1970s, public opinion strongly supported more independence for youth, more distance between parents and kids, and a general rolling back of any *in loco parentis* role.

A quarter-century has passed, and the passage of time has gradually changed Boomer minds about this law. They are no longer FERPA's protected class, but rather the class from whom others are being protected: namely, their own children. Today, it is not uncommon for Boomer parents of Millennial collegians to demand—in the name of truth and justice and fairness—to see their children's private records. The role of parent is sacred to many of them, and they just aren't sure if they can trust a college to replace them in that role.

The controversy hit the news in the spring of 2000, when a superachieving 19-year-old student set herself ablaze in her dorm room at the Massachusetts Institute of Technology. Until her suicide, her parents knew nothing of her inner anguish. Furious that the university never alerted them that a school psychiatrist had considered hospitalizing their daughter, they sued MIT in a case that has drawn national media attention. In mounting a vigorous defense, the college cited its FERPA requirements as protecting it from liability. (A decision is still pending at this writing.)

What can a college do?

Take concrete steps to inform parents and students of FERPA rights and responsibilities, right at the start of the students' college career. Make sure parents know that students may, in writing, waive FERPA rules and allow a parent or guardian to have access to their records. Make the waiver simple, so that every family that wants it gets it. Your goal should be to move the controversy away from the college and back squarely to the student and parent.

Because many students will be inclined to sign waivers, often quite willingly, college information systems must adapt to larger numbers of "open record" students. Academic counselors and health professionals must be aware that any student who walks in the door may have parents who expect to be notified immediately in case of trouble. Counselors should try to keep close relationships with parents and, perhaps, with other professionals who have dealt with students previously.

Could this tension between legal requirements and changing public mores lead to the end of FERPA? Perhaps. Rather than having to deal with different categories of "waivered" and "unwaivered" students, along with legal worries about how specific each waiver must be, colleges may press Congress to relax some FERPA regulations, much as the law has already been amended to allow parental notification in the case of drug or alcohol abuse. Under a relaxed FERPA, however, colleges would have a much clearer burden to keep in touch with parents and may have to increase staff to comply. Each student's health and academic status would have to be monitored, and any warning signs or deviations reported to parents—quite a contrast with the college world that most of today's Boomers recall.

Here again, careful parent management will be one of the most nerve-wracking challenges of the Millennial college era. With or without FERPA, it is the new challenge of today's college administrators to persuade today's parents to "let go," just a little bit more with each passing year, with confidence that their come-of-age Millennial children remain in very good hands.

While Millennials are in most respects the healthiest youths in our nation's history, there are problem areas: ADD and ADHD, asthma, athletic injuries (especially among girls), obesity, and eating disorders. Of these, perhaps the most addressable are eating issues. At one edge, more will come to campus with weight problems, reflecting an increasing trend toward obesity among all age brackets over the last several decades, and may overdue it at eating hall buffets. At the other edge, many will skip meals or delve into harmful food fads or worse (anorexia, bulimia, or "exercise bulimia") out of range of daily parental control. Residence hall assistants should be encouraged to watch for these problems, inquire into student's eating and exercise habits, and where necessary refer students for counseling.

Over their lifetimes, today's teens have broadly been invited to consult with credentialed adults and to rely on their judgment about getting prescriptions for "ailments" that older generations would have borne without complaint. The trend reinforces how Millennials trust institutions and adults, believe in the efficacy of health care science, and have a low tolerance for people (including themselves) who persistently feel bad about life.

On-campus emotional and psychiatric issues will rise in importance, not because Millennials have more emotional problems than prior generations (for the first time in decades, the rate of youth suicide and self-reported depression is now trending down), but because addressing any emotional problems has become a higher priority. More students seek counseling, in high school and college, and many more have psychiatric diagnoses and come to campus with prescriptions for psychotropic medications. This is a mixed blessing for colleges. Thanks to advances in mental health treatment, students who a decade ago might not have attended college can now have successful college careers. At the same time, not just these students but most students—and their parents—will make major new demands on campus counseling and health care services.

From an early age, Millennials have been encouraged to talk over their problems with trusted and credentialed adults, with their parents always getting full reports. In college, they will still search out a sympathetic ear, and will have plenty to talk about when they find it. Moreover, when their college-age child has health problems, physical or emotional, parents will want to know about it, regardless of whether the student might want to keep it secret. Campuses should go out of their way to alert every parent and student to FERPA privacy laws and, if parent and child wish it, have all parties sign the necessary disclosure forms well in advance.

Protections against excessive commercialism will also become part of the new *in loco communitatis* doctrine of collegiate sheltering. When Millennials were in grade school, poster ads, candy machines, soda pouring rights, and net marketing software came under attack from parents and community leaders. Many school districts have responded by giving up those things, and foregoing the extra income. Colleges are about to face a similar choice. Deluxe retailers, mailing list vendors, credit card companies, and pharmaceutical companies want to ply their wares to a vast and affluent new crop of undergrads. Think twice before opening the gate and letting them in, unless you don't mind fielding endless "Is it true that you allow…?" queries from outraged dads, muckraking journalists, and moralizing legislators.

Millennials are used to living in a rule-bound world. More than Boomers and Xers at the same age, they are comfortable with the "broken window" theory of social disorder whereby authorities have "zero tolerance" for even minor infractions. Today's teens may be somewhat more inclined than prior generations to report such infractions—and, when asked, are more likely to say that enforcement does not go far enough. Many would happily participate in student juries, as they have been accustomed to doing since high school days.

## Implications for the Classroom

Just as colleges and universities can expect to be held increasingly accountable for the personal safety of their students, they can also expect increasing scrutiny—from parents, the media, and the government—of what goes on in the classroom. Expect more complaints about "unfair" grades, and even lawsuits over "injurious" academic evaluations, to be filed by disappointed students and their disgruntled parents. Brace for more intrusions from politicians. Virginia is considering legislation that would apply Standards of Learning to the state's public colleges and universities. Just as high school teachers had to submit to performance measures when Millennials were in high school, professors may have to do the same as Millennials pass through college.

Professors will face increasing scrutiny of what values they impart, or appear to impart, in the classroom. In the summer of 2002, a Zogby poll found that 73 percent of college students reported that when their professors taught ethical issues, the usual message was that "right and wrong depends on differences in individual values and cultural diversity." The very commissioning of the poll, along with mass publicity it received, are harbingers of an era in which society at large will be more engaged in the debate over college curricula and the moral education of collegians. Professors could start hearing complaints from parents who differ with their points of view, especially if their collegiate children report back home that they are getting more attitude and opinion than knowledge in the classroom.

Spurred by an intensely interested media, the definition of an appropriate relationship between faculty and undergrads will narrow. The "anything goes" sexual ethos on campus that faculty members may recall from their own undergrad years is now a relic of the past. Not only are Millennials themselves more sexually cautious than were college students during the last four decades, they are the objects of heightened parental and societal concern over every aspect of their well-being, including their romantic lives.

# 8 | Confident

"This is the first time in history of the human race that a generation of kids has overtaken their parents in the use of new technology."

— PETER EIO, LEGO SYSTEMS (2000)

# Confident

Today's collegians are far more upbeat, often robustly so, than any batch seen in many decades. In a 1999 Public Agenda survey, 90 percent of teens said they are personally happy and excited about their future. That's how they were in high school, and it's carrying over into college.

Most Millennials would subscribe to that old 4-H slogan, "To Make the Best Bester." According to a new Bayer/Gallop "Facts of Science" survey, 84 percent of college students believe they are "science literate," 86 percent believe someone in their own generation will become the next Bill Gates, 66 percent believe they personally know such a person, and fully one quarter believe that they actually are that person. Yet when asked if they wished they had a stronger preparation in math and science before they entered college, 40 percent of respondents said "yes," and three in five felt they had not had the preparation they need.

More than Boomers or Gen Xers at the same age, Millennials like to apply their analytic skills to thinking through the long-term consequences of personal choices and acquired habits. This helps explain why youths are turning away from so many types of behavioral risk-taking (such as pregnancies, substance abuse, and crime). It also helps explain why so many teens complain about stress in their lives.

## Implications for Recruiting and Admissions

"This is your brain; this is your brain on drugs" was a line in a famous early '90s anti-drug ad targeting Gen Xers. "Tell me you're proud of me" is a line from a new ad targeting Millennials. This juxtaposition demonstrates the stark difference in how recruiting messages should be re-crafted, and re-targeted, as the one generation has given way to the other. The logic of the old message was damage control: Tell teens about the horrible things that will happen if they don't make the right choice. The logic of the new message is positive reinforcement: Tell teens about the great things that will happen if they make the right choice.

Recruiting materials should not dwell on how your college can provide a backstop and help students manage their problems. Instead, describe your institution as a place where young people realize their dreams and where most students are capable of wonders. Today's high school teens don't need to be reminded that success requires hard work—and that sometimes even hard work doesn't pan out. Stress that your institution offers a place where great students go, not simply to improve themselves or prepare for a career, but to meet and work and develop lifelong friendships with other very capable students.

## Implications for Campus Life

The "rah-rah" spirit of campus life recalled by today's senior citizens is on track to return. Though it may disturb faculty members who during their own college years voiced counter-cultural dissent, many Millennials will reveal what their edgier elders might demean as "corny-cultural" values. Today's collegians may find nothing inauthentic about college spirit—in a modernized rebirth of pep rallies, awards ceremonies, school songs, proms, and the like. Instead, they'll find in such activities a therapeutic release from the stress of achievement and a cathartic expression of solidarity. The class of 2007 will have a much stronger sense of its generational identity than the class of 1997, and will want to engage in ceremonies and activities that reinforce a sense of collective destiny.

# Emotional Depression

Because Millennials are pressured, more incoming freshmen than ever (28 percent) report "frequently feeling overwhelmed." Because they expect their bad feelings to be ministered to, more freshmen than ever (6 percent) say they "probably will use personal counseling" while at college. And because a rising share have already taken prescription medications for emo-tional problems while in grade school, more are taking them in college. Thanks to such medications, many students can now enroll in college who never would have applied before. One unsurprising result is that 85 percent of college coun-seling centers report a rise in the number of students with "severe psychological problems"—versus 56 percent in 1988.

It does not follow, however, that Millennials in general are more emotion-ally depressed and troubled than earlier student cohorts. To the contrary, the share of incoming freshmen who report "frequently feeling depressed" reached a record low (7.8 percent) in 2001. Nor is it true that youth rates of suicide are rising. They are falling.

| Table 2 | Averages | |
|---|---|---|
| | 1990–1996 | 2001 |
| Share of freshmen who say they are "frequently overwhelmed" | 23.5% | 28.0% |
| Share of freshmen who say they will likely seek "personal counseling" | 3.7% | 6.6% |
| Share of freshmen who say they are "frequently depressed" | 9.3% | 7.8% |
| U.S. suicides per 100,000, aged 15–19 | 10.7 | 8.7 |
| U.S. suicides per 100,000, aged 20–24 | 15.4 | 12.8 |

At the same time, administrators and faculty members are likely to be confronted with new forms of student intolerance that will create new challenges. Millennials do not seem as committed as prior youth genera-tions to the precepts of free speech. However, their interpretation of what is and is not allowable speech will not always fit within what many in the 1990s came to call "political correctness." More so than with older Americans, the Millennials' pre-existing urge to reinvent the civic order was augmented by the events of 9/11 and its aftermath. As a group, they are likely to shift the balance in the old campus debate between civic duty and freedom of expression. This is a trend that many college administrators and faculty members may find quite disturbing.

## Implications for the Classroom

Millennials are collectively confident about their future, which means they perceive greater dangers, and fewer rewards, in any attempt to be creatively different from their peers. Following the rules, working really hard, not messing up—that's the common Millennial credo. One hears less talk about winning or standing out.

This new batch of students will be less comfortable working independently and will reveal a tendency toward safety in number—toward conformity—that may be distressing to professors who may recall a very different classroom environment in the 1960s or '70s. Many high school teachers lament that they can't get their students to debate an issue where they already feel a strong consensus. Professors will have to go to extra efforts to tap into the latent creativity of students who, having been "taught to the test," are unfamiliar with taking intellectual risks.

This tendency to risk aversion is worsened by grade inflation. When all smart students are presumed to get A's, a student can only lose by taking a risk with a creative paper that might not appeal to an opinionated professor or an experimental project that does not come to a neat conclusion.

Finding a way to fix grade inflation, and clear out some extra room for students to demonstrate high degrees of excellence, has become an issue at many colleges. At Harvard, where until recently more than half of all grades were A's, one hears new vows to "crack down," and hard-working students at harder-grading colleges are understandably resentful when they hear of the high marks routinely given to students elsewhere—students who, come grad school application time, will be their competitors.

The problem is, how does a college fix a devalued currency without going through a long period of demoralizing adjustment? To borrow an analogy from monetary currencies, one solution may be simply to switch to a different currency. For example, the faculty could switch over to a non-letter-grade system, or invent a grade or honor higher than A, to make a regular A the equivalent of what a B or B+ used to be.

# 9 | Team-Oriented

"We're seeing a huge cultural shift away from the word 'I' to the word 'We' in this new generation of young people coming in. And that's to be celebrated."

— GENERAL JAMES JONES, U.S. MARINE CORPS COMMANDANT (2002)

# Team-Oriented

From pre-school through high school, from Barney and select soccer to school juries and collaborative learning, Millennials have been developing strong team instincts and tight peer bonds. No Boomer or Gen Xer could visit a high school classroom over the last several years without being impressed by the new emphasis on teamwork. Students learn in groups, deliver presentations in groups, and get graded in groups. They review each other's assignments and supervise each other's behavior. They form teams to volunteer for community projects.

Meanwhile, the expression "peer pressure" is gaining a newly positive connotation. Social marketers now find that safety or antidrug messages which tell teens to improve their behavior so as not to let a friend down often work better than messages that target a teenager's own self-interest. Through the 1990s, a rising share of high school seniors have said that "staying close to friends" (as well as "parents") will be a high priority, after graduation.

Between morning classes, Millennials can be seen on cellphones, keeping in close touch with friends on campus or back home. At the end of the school day, Millennials use the Internet to stay in constant contact with a larger circle of friends via chat rooms and buddy lists. In some respects, the very tightness of these circles of friends, as reinforced by these new technologies, is making it harder for Millennials to "let go" of their old high school worlds, to replace old friends with new ones.

## Implications for Recruiting and Admissions

College recruiters must learn how to take advantage of the strong role of peer pressure among Millennials. Military recruiters are already doing it. Historically, the armed forces have defined the term "influencers" to mean parents, relatives of military lineage, and teachers. But these days, successful recruiting sergeants know a lot about the interactions of their teenage prospects, and they understand how avid they can be as followers. If one of the coolest seniors in a school decides to be a recruit, it has a real ripple effect, drawing many others in the direction of military service. This makes the followers look hard, and wonder, 'Geez, is that for me? If Justin's doing it…'

Conformity may be the shadow side of the Millennial Generation, but it is undeniably a powerful motivator. More than Gen Xers, Millennials place a high value in going to the same college as their high school buddies. (Back in the 1960s, many Boomers preferred to go to colleges attended by no one they knew.) As the appeal of "making it on your own" dwindles, college recruiters should think anew about how teens influence each other in making life decisions.

Many colleges are already using enrollment management systems, designed to maximize overall student retention, that implicitly harness peer influence. Instead of focusing exclusively on prospects with the highest GPAs, for example, enrollment management software can focus on very good but not superior students (say, with 3.3 to 3.5 GPAs) from specific regions or with certain nonscholastic interests or achievements as the best way to build a more cohesive and loyal student body.

**Figure 16 ▶**

Male Share of Total Students Enrolled in U.S. Institutions of Higher Learning, 1947–1999

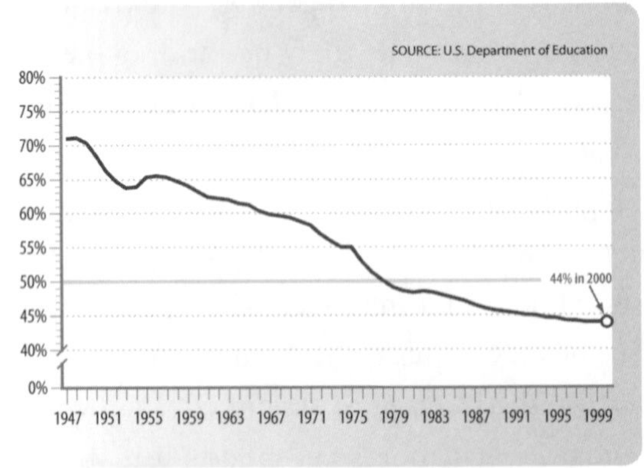

SOURCE: U.S. Department of Education

44% in 2000

At first hesitantly, and now quite openly, many colleges have begun seeking more male applicants. The past decade has seen a steadily increasing advantage in the number of female over male college applicants, under-grads, and graduates. Coming out of high school, fewer men than women apply for college; of those, fewer men are accepted; and of those, more men drop out in their freshmen and sophomore year. Fully 58 percent of all college freshmen are now women, a proportion that is rising by the year. At many liberal arts colleges, and for black students nationwide, the female share is roughly 65 percent—very different from Boomer college days, when men greatly outnumbered women, and the minority gender shares were close to 50-50.

Underlying this imbalance is a growing gap in academic achievement. Men score as well as (or better than) women in pure aptitude tests, but by nearly every measure of applied effort women now come out on top. Of the roughly 750,000 teens in the 1997 *Who's Who Among American High School Students*, nearly two-thirds were girls—and, among those listed, girls were twice as likely as boys to have "A" grade averages. Summarizing the data, the Horatio Alger Association's "State of Our Nation's Youth" report concluded: "Females challenged themselves more frequently to take the most difficult courses available…[and] worked harder at their course work and received better grades than males." Anyone who today peruses a high school yearbook, or visits a high school awards assembly or honors class, will be struck by the preponderance of girls.

In many ways, the rise of Millennial women represents a triumph of feminism. Much of what once may have been controversial about the higher education and professional aspirations of women is now accepted as a given, by young women and men alike.

Yet a growing gender achievement gap is not a trend that can be sustained indefinitely—and even if it were, it conceals a gender perception

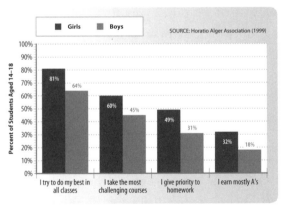

◀ **Figure 17**

Survey of Students Aged 14–18 in 1998 to 1999, Answers by Gender

gap that does pose real problems for college recruiters. With all the new stress on teamwork and social skills and "zero tolerance" of what some might call typical boy behavior, young Millennial males feel at a disadvantage—and by the time they leave high school, many develop an aversion to educators who (they think) regard them primarily as problems. Even bright and energetic young men often search for alternatives (military service, free-lancing, business start-ups) to anything resembling more "school."

Recruiters who want to attract more men must understand that their first challenge is to break the "school" mold. They need to demonstrate how the challenges and payoffs of their institution—everything from the intellectual excitement it offers to the character transformation it promises—is entirely unlike "school" as many high school boys have known it. Recruiters can press the case that their college confers long-term economic advantages beyond those now available in such newly popular post-high school male environments as the armed services and technology companies. They should also explicitly target men who are eager to enter college after spending two or three years "settling down" in one of these alternative settings.

Where the gender equation has mostly just shifted, since the days of Boomer collegians, the race equation has become far more complex. Compared with their parents at the same age, Millennial teens interact socially with teens of other races much more frequently—and, as a group, are much more optimistic about the future of race relations. A visitor to today's campus will still notice racial cliques, in eating halls or elsewhere, but this is a social environment that Millennials inherited, not one that they created.

More than their parents at the same age, Millennials are bothered by preferential admissions quotas or formulas based on race. One reason may be that today's teens, aware of the growing and immigrant-boosted diversity of races among their peers, don't believe that simple yes-no categories can possibly match racial reality any more. Another reason may be the rapidly rising number of affluent nonwhite households, in particular the high visibility of numerous very wealthy nonwhite athletes and other celebrities—all of which erodes, in teens' eyes, the old association between minority race and social disadvantage. Whatever the reason, preferential rules on race strike many of today's collegians as less about equal opportunity than simply about race *per se*—and, thus, sit uncomfortably with this generation's "fair play" ethic.

The bottom line is that most Millennial teens see racial diversity on campus—including living with and working with students of other races—as a hugely appealing part of their college experience. They believe it helps unlock something very important and positive that their generation has to offer, and recruiters should highlight this aspect of what their institutions can provide. Yet they should do it in a Millennial style, which means embracing a wide new diversity of racial definitions and no longer pigeonholing

> **Millennial Attitudes Toward Affirmative Action**
>
> Asked nationally of 2001 freshman class:
> **"Affirmative action in college admissions should be abolished."**
>   49% agree "strongly" or "somewhat"
>   (*The American Freshman*, UCLA, 2001)
>
> Asked of University of Michigan student body:
> **"Do you support or object to the use of race as a factor in undergraduate admissions?"**
>   51% object
>   41% support
>   (*Michigan Daily*, April 19, 1999)
>
> 1,600 teens in online poll:
> **"Do you agree with using affirmative action as a factor in college admissions?"**
>   81% no
>   19% yes
>   (*Teen People*, September 2001)

races into fixed cultural or economic boxes. Millennials believe more in a "transracial" than a "multiracial" society. The image should be more of blended pigments than white next to black, of dozens of races cooperating rather than two or three races pulling in different directions.

As social activism among Millennials grows in cohesion and effectiveness, it will increasingly target issues of class and income, rather than gender or race. Collegiate efforts to reposition affirmative action as an income- rather than a race-based policy may meet with favor among high school seniors. Well before high school graduation, Millennials are becoming aware of the widening gaps that separate families by income and of the unequal struggle among parents to finance their children's education. They also notice that public and private tuition assistance is gradually leaning more to achievement and less to need.

This Millennial money issue guarantees that complaints about tuition hikes and student loans are sure to rise in the years ahead. Over the last twenty years, the average college tuition—public and private—has risen considerably faster than inflation or average household income, making college a greater economic burden on families than they were when Gen X began entering college in the '80s and certainly since Boomers began entering college in the '60s. The growing disparity in household incomes combined with the larger share of teens wanting to go to college has ramped up the demand for means-tested financial aid and scholarships. Meanwhile, affluent midlife parents are nowhere near as inclined as before to trust college administrators to redistribute a sizeable share of their tuition money (on average, an estimated 38% of the full tuition at a private college) however they see fit. The bottom line result is a rising and heated controversy over the size and purpose of tuition "discounting."

So much negotiating and discounting is going on now that students (and their parents) worry more than before about where the game ends

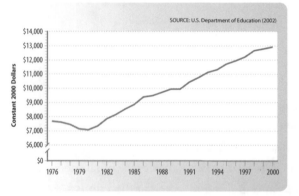

**Figure 18 ▶**

Average Annual Tuition, Room, and Board in Constant 2000 Dollars at 4-Year Institutions of Higher Learning, 1976 to 2000

and the rules begin. When the media refer to college tuitions as "sticker prices," no one can be surprised when many "sticker-shocked" parents try to seek a better deal. When aid is no longer based on clear and simple criteria, no one can blame a student and parent who, upon leaving a financial aid interview, feel like airline passengers in an age of air fare lotto, restricted discounts, and frequent flyer programs. Are they paying too much? Can they save another thousand dollars by making one phone call, getting a counteroffer from a rival, and leveraging that into a new tuition deal?

Tuition discounting is on just one of the two sides of the budget squeeze institutions will face in the Millennial era. The other side—where and how to spend money, where and how to cut back—will be just as contentious.

Many colleges may have to choose between whether they wish to compete on the basis of quality (from single dorm rooms to small classes) or on the basis of price. Some colleges may quality-compete with better facilities (dorms, teched-up classrooms, gyms, theaters), others compete with more faculty time and attention. To improve their position, some larger institutions may try to find ways of openly detaching the receipts and expenditures of the undergraduate teaching ("college") side from those of the research ("university") side.

Whatever colleges do to compete, they will need to pitch new recruiting messages about how they can provide greater value for the tuition dollar—messages aimed primarily at parents, but also at students. To the extent these messages call implicit attention to a college's effort to compensate for differences in family wealth or income, they may resonate quite favorably with Millennial teens.

## Implications for Campus Life

Millennials love group work, cooperative activities like volunteer service, and participation in something larger than the individual. For Boomers, community service was often an alternative to getting drafted to go to Vietnam. For Gen Xers, it was often a punishment for various misbehaviors. For Millennials, by contrast, it's the norm—an expected part of anyone's educational experience. This new youth attitude can provide colleges with an enormous opportunity to create a vibrant and exciting campus life. The flip side is: Colleges that fail to do so will have difficulty recruiting and retaining good students.

As Millennials enter college, they will start voting and participating in political activities, much more energetically than Gen X students did through the 1980s and '90s. More students will volunteer, more political clubs will start, more campaign signs will appear, more candidates will visit, and more classroom discussions will drift to politics and current events. As elections near, students will accept their civic duty to vote and will appreciate help in securing absentee ballots from home.

Student governments (and judiciaries) will assume new importance, especially if college administrators expand their authority over student rules, discipline, campus activities, and community service. To this point, Millennial girls have dominated high school student governments and can be expected to do likewise in college (perhaps prepping for the day this generation provides the U.S. with its first female President).

The new Millennial focus on community building will redefine race and ethnicity as campus issues. Boomers and Gen Xers attended college when immigration was on the rise—an age of "multiculturalism" when racial differences were celebrated and ethnic separateness asserted. Millennials, by contrast, are more often *second*-generation immigrants, more assimilation-minded, and more likely to focus on what people of different races have in common.

Each year, as more Millennials enter college, self-segregating dorms, clubs, and eating areas will become less popular and more controversial—even repellent to many potential applicants. While Millennials are far less Caucasian (and far more Latino) than any other generation in U.S. history, so too are they far more likely to be—or aspire for their children to be—mixed race. Since today's teens widely believe they handle racial issues better than older people, they will not take well to being lectured to, or chastised, about these subjects.

As issues of race and ethnicity may become less important on campus, issues of income or wealth—as is the case with recruiting—will become more so. Where their Boomer parents grew up in times of relatively narrow class distinctions, Millennials have grown up in a world in which class divisions have grown wider by the year. By the time they arrive in college, Millennial understand that some students will be able to flaunt the enormous resources they receive from parents, while others will face obvious challenges just making ends meet. By some accounts, teens in today's high schools are more likely to date a member of another race than a person of significantly higher or lower economic standing. Students with fewer financial resources—those who have to work or carry the largest loans—often find their burdens embarrassing and try to cover them up as much as they can.

To alleviate class distinctions on campus, a college can guard against a possible money bias in the admissions process (for example, in early decision and alumni advantage), dorm and food choices, campus activities, and selection of fields of study or specific classes (by resisting demands from the parents of "full freight" students to enjoy privileges not extended to other students). The proliferation of cars is a very visible symbol of the widening economic gap between students, and a college can put students on a more common plane by imposing schoolwide car limits, restricting parking, or replacing parking fines with requirements for community service. Financial aid counselors should monitor the year-to-year financial circumstance of lower-income students to make sure that no student suffers a crushing work or debt load.

But if Millennial teens are part of this money problem, they also see themselves as key to its long-term solution. They may eventually organize major political and economic movements to correct them, much in the way Boomers, having grown up in an era of sharp gender and race differences, later took major steps to narrow those differences.

As Millennials mobilize, they might begin with on-campus campaigns. Millennial collegians might make energetic advocates on behalf of junior faculty members and low-wage campus workers who complain about pay or working conditions. "Living wage" demands could become more widespread, and effective. In time, Millennial collegians may propel a new unionism on campus and fuel a class-based agenda whose object will directly clash with the goal of tuition reduction. As the Millennials pass through college propelling these and other political movements, some campus administrators may yearn for the "good old days" when collegians cared more about cultural or ethnic awareness issues and less about economic and political organizing.

Amid the rebirth of campus community that Millennials are likely to bring, campus officials must be mindful of loners. According to countless surveys, teenagers have become more relationship-dependent over the past decade. They value friendships more, spend less time alone, and pay more attention to peer opinion. This results in a more cliquish, rule-oriented social world—a world in which cooperation is prized, looking after your circle of friends is priority number one, and being "nice" is esteemed. Yet it is also a world in which social outsiders—the bullied boy or the snubbed girl—can feel greater pain.

Many colleges already struggle to help students who can't find a niche or social identity on campus. In the past, those students suffered mostly loneliness. In the Millennial era, they may also suffer ostracism or even feelings of violent alienation. One of the lessons of Columbine and the other dramatic school shootings of the 1990s is that, amid this very social generation, those who don't fit in can suffer inordinately, and in extreme cases can become very dangerous.

This last challenge is overwhelmingly a male problem and is connected to a larger issue that will face institutions of higher learning: After male undergrads are recruited, how can they be retained? Many options are available, but all of them should focus on creating or expanding male "bastions" on campus in which young men will be encouraged to apply their masculinity in socially constructive ways. These may include closer campus links to such male-dominated career arenas as officer training and the high-tech information industry.

## Implications for the Classroom

The Millennial group ethic will require substantial changes in how classrooms are run. On the one hand, many students may expect team teaching and team grading of team projects. Professors who can do this will gain a measure of approval and enthusiasm from students. Teaching techniques that combine teamwork and technology, especially in the applied sciences, may yield spectacular results.

Getting Millennials to apply themselves over a sustained period to an independent or creative task will require careful thought and classroom planning. Having students debate or critique each other's work (an approach that typically energized Boomer students) is a difficult challenge that often misfires among Millennials, especially when staged before an entire class. A better strategy is to have students perform independent assignments in a framework that requires them, at some final stage, to integrate all the work into some collaborative output.

The Millennial team ethic will also influence student preferences among academic disciplines. Faculties should expect declining interest in preparation for business entrepreneurship and increasing interest in public service. A poll by Hart-Teeter, conducted in April 2002 on behalf of the Council for Excellence in Government, found that 40 percent of young adults aged 18 to 30 say that a career in government is very or fairly appealing to them. This is up five percentage points since 1997. Even more striking is how the motivations of those attracted to public service have changed. In 1997 a 53 percent majority said that good compensation and job security were the most appealing features of government service, compared with 40 percent who cited either helping people or serving their community or country. In 2002, the motivations were reversed—with 54 percent naming helping people or serving the community as the top reasons for service, with just 42 percent looking to compensation or job security.

Millennials will want to learn how to apply technology to big social problems like global warming and world governance. As befits a generation that grew up with computer and video games in which they designed "Sim Cities" and built "Civilizations," they will show rising interest in practical questions of political, social, and economic management and a declining interest in theoretical research that lacks world-changing applications. Millennials may reveal a diminished interest in identity politics, but exercises that appeal to their role as citizens will enable them to apply their growing desire to be active in mainstream political parties and causes, much as the generation of collegians did back in the 1930s.

Ethnic studies will retain plenty of interest to members of a generation this diverse, but they can be expected to change focus, with less student interest in the black-and-white dialogue building that dominated the era in which many of these programs were launched. Interest in the social sciences, including macroeconomics, government, and political science, can be expected to grow.

Interest in gender studies is likely to wane. For this generation, on the whole, feminism is less a *cause* than a *given*, and one that needs some fixing. The young Boomer challenge was to promote sexual independence by trashing social norms. The young Millennial challenge is to enable sexual *dependence* by energizing social norms, including modesty, courtship, and monogamy. Indeed, for Millennials, one of the biggest emerging gender issues is how high-earning women and lesser-earning men will, when married, bear the high opportunity cost of one spouse staying home to raise children.

Faculty would do well to remember that the various causes of the 1960s, which to many (liberal or conservative) have remained lodestars, are as chronologically distant from today's Millennials as World War I and Prohibition were to Boomers when they were in college. Faculty who envision Millennials as instruments for completing their "half-finished" societal agendas may come away disappointed, frustrated, and deeply critical of these new youth for the "lessons" they have supposedly "forgotten"—when, in fact, the real lesson of history is that generations, like time itself, must always move on.

# 10 | Conventional

"Perhaps reacting to what might be described as the excesses of their parents' generation, teens today are decidedly more traditional than their elders were, in both lifestyles and attitudes."

— GEORGE GALLUP, JR., THE GALLUP ORGANIZATION (2002)

# Conventional

If there ever were an archetype for the conventional side of the Millennial generation, it's Harry Potter. In newspaper movie sections, the typical film shot of Harry shows a bright-eyed boy in glasses looking very proper in a uniform dress shirt and tie. This primness resonates with younger Millennials, as do many other features of Harry Potter's world. It features a group of kids who struggle to excel and have fun in a very structured institutional environment. (They worry a lot about grades and exams and punishments and penalties.) They look up to a teaching faculty filled with wise but eccentric middle-aged spiritualists. And, from time to time, the kids have to band together to save the universe from total destruction. Except for very evil people, no one feels fundamentally alienated or oppressed. And there is no ambiguity about who those very evil people are.

## Implications for Recruiting and Admissions

Far more than Gen Xers or Boomers before them, Millennials believe in big brands. Whether choosing clothes, cars, or colleges, they tend to go with the group. Are Harvard, Yale, and Princeton the top three Ivies? Then that's where the top students want to go. Is the big state university in the famous college town the place everybody at school is talking about? Then that's where everybody else wants to go.

Today, as in the 1930s, the era of the "regular" student is coming back. All recruiters should ask, "Are good solid students with conventional values welcome at our college?" At some campuses, many teens might easily get the impression that such students are not—and that the only students who are welcome are those who are odd or peculiar or unique. "Colleges are not really looking at individuals anymore," Richard Reeves has sardonically observed. "They are trying to build 'a community'—and for that they need a violinist and a muscleman, someone pious and someone devious, perhaps even a village idiot." That's an increasingly common complaint one hears from today's high school seniors, sharpened by the Millennial desire to be conventional, non-confrontational, and not stick out too much from the pack.

These new mixed feelings about assertions of individualism are one reason why many high school seniors regard essay questions on college application forms as a sham. Cheating on them is widespread, ranging from the petty to the serious, from having mom and dad help out with punctuation to hiring professional wordsmiths to invent all the breathless verbiage about struggle and awakening and inner triumph that Millennials are told college admissions committees want to hear.

Beyond the reactions of Millennial teens themselves, there is the deeper question of what the essays are meant to reveal: conventional competence in composition, or originality of experience and expression? If a college conveys that it is looking for the latter, many Millennials will find this disturbing. What's wrong with being conventional, many may think, if it means trying to live up to a common and widely held standard of good behavior? Today's teens often associate excessive individualism with social dysfunction, or perhaps, as in Harry Potter's world, with evil. Even if they can get in to a college full of unconventional people, they might not want to go there.

The Millennial era looks to be one in which big new collegiate brands can be created, in the minds of young people who want to identify the new mainstream, meet its standard, and brand themselves for life as a smart and capable person.

## Implications for Campus Life

Millennials begin with a high level of respect for institutions, but with that respect come very high expectations. They count on adults to be exemplars. An individual professor, or administrator, who fails to live up to those expectations will lose a great deal of trust—and may find it very difficult to earn it back. Millennials grew up during a period of "zero tolerance" for youthful misbehavior, yet also a period in which adults in positions of authority (in government, business, academe, the church, and elsewhere) were held far less accountable for any misbehavior of their own. Preserving academic freedom is important, but administrators who fail to remove incompetent or unprepared professors—or any faculty members who engage in sexual harassment, use drugs, or pursue fraudulent research— risk the danger of unprecedented backlash from students and parents.

In many ways, what today's parents remember of the sexual revolution is coming full circle. In the Boomer youth era, more went on than adults thought. Now, in the Millennial era, less is going on than adults think. "It's funny," said Sarah Brown, director of the National Campaign to Prevent Teen Pregnancy, commenting on the continuing decline in the rates of teen abortion and pregnancy. "Never has anxiety been higher about bare midriffs and all-night raves. But kids are having less sex, and those who do are using contraceptives much more carefully."

### Where Have All the Streakers Gone?

News Item: More than 4,000 University of Michigan students lined the streets of Ann Arbor on April 19th, 2002 in hopes of seeing the bare flesh of runners sprinting during the annual Naked Mile. Started as a prank by the crew and lacrosse teams in the late 1980s, this annual rite of Spring attracted between 800 and 1,000 runners four years ago and more than 12,000 onlookers. But this year, only about 20 students even attempted to make the run, and many of those who did were prevented by heavy police presence from taking it all off.

Back in the 1970s, Boomer kids called it "streaking"—a daring exhibitionist display by one fast-running loner. In the '80s, groups of college-age Xers took this derring-do to another level. The first Naked Mile was run in 1986. Its popularity rose to stellar heights in the mid-90s, but faded fast over the last few years—especially after the original crew and lacrosse sponsors began boycotting the event in 2000. Why the fade? The university and local law enforcement became stricter about enforcing rules and laws. More students began worrying about parents finding out, about blemishes on their record, and about having their bodies filmed and broadcast on the Internet. And many upper-classmen now say that when they first witnessed the event as freshmen they were simply grossed out by the whole thing.

Part of the adult misimpression about Millennials and sex arises from their frequent brashness when talking or writing about the subject. (One foreign journalist recently described American high school girls as "vulgar virgins.") Some students have begun publishing explicit sex columns for college papers, even as these writers remain private about their own sexual experience. Had these columns appeared in the 1960s or '70s, they would have been part of a youth rebellion, out of step with the adult world. Today, these columns fit right into the adult world Millennials have been intently watching, in the news and in the culture, ever since they reached puberty.

The same shift in generational experience applies to vulgarity. As a group, Millennial teens use more vulgar words than teens of past generations, but they're less likely to use original vulgarities than those that older culture creators (mostly Gen Xers) have crafted for them. One analysis of teen profanity discovered that 80 percent of their vulgar utterances were directly borrowed from pop songs or films. And where, back in the '60s, Boomers were more provocative than the culture, today's teens are less provocative. Older ears must also keep in mind that language does change and re-norm, and that words (like "sucks") that sound vulgar to the old do not to the young—and, at times (as in words like "shag"), the reverse is true.

Like other generations, Millennial collegians will make the most out of being young, and that includes sex and slang—but unlike other generations, they will take more cues and follow rules of older adults, as long as those cues and rules don't involve double standards. If college administrators or faculty advisors would like to tone down a sex column in a college paper, or set language rules for a college radio station, Millennials might grumble a little at first but are likely to oblige in the end—as long as the same rules will apply to what professors say in classrooms and write in academic journals.

On the whole, Millennials are more willing to accept adult authority than Boomer or Gen X collegians used to do. They are a generation that can be led, whether by an administration seeking to impose new dress codes, or by junior faculty and support staff seeking higher pay, or by off-campus organizers promoting any number of causes. For better or for worse, expect major power plays among adults competing for the allegiance of Millennial troops. And brace for the "orders" being more controversial among adults, especially faculty members, than among student bodies.

## Implications for the Classroom

Once upon a time, young Boomers believed that no one was telling "the truth" in America—and they felt it was their duty to pronounce it. Today, Millennials are more inclined to accept that nearly everyone is telling "the truth" about something, and they feel their duty is to impose some sort of order on the resulting hurricane of information. In this context, what's important about a history paper or customized CD or community service web site is less its originality than its usefulness in simplifying the world and making life more manageable.

These Millennial agendas will attract plenty of complaints from middle-aged people of a self-professed "creative" bent—including many academics. In a torrent of responses to David Brooks' April 2001 *Atlantic* cover story, "The Organization Kid," today's collegians were pelted with descriptors like robotic, sheep, conformist, mechanical, eunuchs, shallow, and so on—comments written by Boomers and Gen Xers who came of age when (supposedly) prophets made of truer stuff strode the earth.

This has all the ingredients of a new generation gap, on campus and elsewhere. Boomers are no longer young activists; Millennials have to fill that role. And, just like Boomer parents, Boomer faculty may struggle a little as they learn (or are taught) to "let go." Many of today's collegians will bristle at professors who condescend to them, or who lay claim to greater personal authenticity, or who can't set aside old crusades that young collegians may regard as simply irrelevant, or who see in today's collegians nothing more than instruments for completing their own half-finished agendas.

Yet, in this new era as in any other, a college faculty has a duty to challenge the self-impression of youth. In the emerging Millennial mindset, it seems useless to be an "original" whom no one will imitate—or a "leader" whom no one will follow. Professors must challenge these assumptions, while being mindful, sometimes even respectful, of the generational experience that has made them so pronounced.

# 11 | Pressured

"Sometimes I feel more pressure than maybe I should, because I know there are so many people who want me to do well."

— SARAH HUGHES, AGE 16, ON HER 2002 OLYMPIC VICTORY

# Pressured

There's a new "arms race" among today's teens, and it's called: "Getting Into College." According to recent surveys, the two items that worry teenagers the most these days are grades and college admissions. (Twenty-five years ago, the most worrisome items in a teen's world were the twin threats of nuclear war and stagflation; a decade ago, they were AIDS and violent crime.)

Millennials are feeling academic stress in ways Boomers and Gen Xers could not have imagined at the same age. Employers are asking to see high school transcripts, test scores, even attendance records. Grades have become more serious than ever. Social promotions are under fire. More homework is being assigned in the younger grades. Recesses and P.E. are disappearing. Class periods are lengthening. Nervous students are

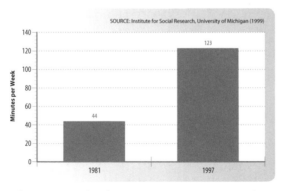

SOURCE: Institute for Social Research, University of Michigan (1999)

◄ **Figure 19**

Average Time Spent per Week on Homework by Students Aged 6–8, 1981 and 1997

turning to a rapidly expanding network of tutoring companies (such as Sylvan, Score!, and the Japanese Kumon Math & Reading Centers, which alone number 1,400 in North America). School years are being extended. Summers are newly serious, with teens packing off to academic camps, and summer schools bursting with mandatory attendees. In 1993, 577,000 students in grades 9 and 10 took the PSAT—a number that by 2001 had jumped to 993,000.

All this pressure has led to an intense emphasis on planning. More than Gen Xers, who excelled at improvisation and at tackling short-term problems, many Millennials have five- or ten-year plans. Millennials see too many adults around them—Gen Xer and Boomer alike—whose lives are a jangle of shards on "sequentially-challenged" life-paths. Too many options at age 21, too many roommates at age 32, and why is Dad worrying about retirement and IRAs when he's only 53?

This experience leads many Millennials to seek security, stability—and, above all, balance—in life's arrangements. Accustomed to Boomer parents whose often chaotic work lives (due to self-employment, contracting, and rapid job turnover), Millennials are far more interested than Gen Xers in institutions, including colleges, that can enhance job and life stability.

## Implications for Recruiting

Many colleges have noted the growing number of applicants who have, from the time they were in elementary school, geared their lives toward getting into "the right college." As more and more students fall into this "over-prepared" category, admissions decisions will become tougher and more competitive—further fueling the cycle of pressure.

There are ways to counteract this. Recruitment materials can convey to students that an institution fits into a life plan, while also offering a place of refuge. While many Millennials seek challenge, most also yearn for a place that allows them a little relief from the intense pressures that society has placed upon them—a long-awaited chance to explore life beyond the next test, the next sporting event, the next music recital, the next science competition. College can get them at least partly out from under overprotective, overly intrusive parents. College is where they can learn to become a whole person, to progress from a scrutinized, pressured childhood to a more balanced and independent adulthood.

To students with this in mind, the best preparation that a college can give is less about vocational training, or even about higher learning, than about helping them acquire the values, habits and skills that will craft them into the kind of adults that they wish to be— adults that are more structured, balanced, and responsible than Millennials believe their own parents to be.

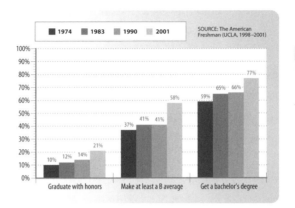

◀ **Figure 20**

National U.S. Freshmen Survey, Expectations for College

## Implications for Campus Life

While Millennials accept academic challenges, they are prone to suffer occasional periods of "burnout." Many never learned to create a suitable balance between work and play. On today's campus, the word "balance" is often heard but less often achieved. Some students realize it's a problem and want to fix it. Others forge on, in ways older people may find both impressive and oppressive, pleasing and disturbing. According to the UCLA Freshman Poll, a record share of new students report feeling so "over-whelmed" that they have sought counseling.

Sleep deficit disorders have posed a serious recent problem among high school students—and can be expected to pose problems in college too. There are three contributing causes: a habit of irregular meals and hours learned from always-on-the-go parents; over-scheduling, learned from perfectionist parents, with the result that the student's meager "down time" comes at the expense of sleep; and inadequate physical exercise. The irregular eating may be too ingrained a life habit to change, but colleges can combat the over-scheduling by moving away from early morning classes, the lack of exercise by offering numerous physical activities, includ-ing intramural sports, for students who might not be so good at them (and, hence, who need them the most).

This last task is best done not by building conventional gyms of the kind that so appealed to Gen Xers, with dozens of individual exercise "stations" enabling each person to work on his or her own program. Such activity can feel entirely solo and interior, subjectively meaningful, but having zero impact on the world. What Millennials would prefer, in an exercise program, is the reverse: something team-oriented with social ritual and huge secular goals. Forget that Boomer health mantra, "It's not the destination, it's the journey." Millennials prefer not to go anywhere until they know the destination.

Look for ways to create stress-free "chill zones" on campus—quiet, out-of-way places where students can gather to play high-tech video games, or low-tech ping pong or pinball, or just sit on cushy couches and watch videos in small groups—and make such zones available as close to 24/7 as possible.

Among the best stress-alleviators will be extra-curricular activities, from fine arts to publications to intramural sports. Students can obsess (and lose sleep) over these too, so the challenge for colleges will be to prompt students to dabble in and explore new things they might never have done before, without the pressure of full commitment or any need to excel or impress anybody. Collegians know that extracurriculars play a very small role in grad school admissions and none at all in the financial aid they may later be offered. Except for the rare few who see extracurriculars as a path to a high-paying pro career—for example, football or basketball players in major college conferences—the pressure will be off.

From college on, Millennials will be pursuing their own dreams, not their parents'.

## Implications for the Classroom

Any discussion of pressure soon leads to the issue of cheating. It is often taken for granted that student cheating has become vastly more commonplace today than it was a generation or two ago. In formal exam situations, no one really knows whether students are cheating more or less than others used to do. There isn't much evidence—and what little there is (of self-reported cheating by college students as far back as 1963) remains ambiguous. According to one recent Gallup report, a steadily *declining* share of 13- to 17-year-olds answering "yes" to the question, "Have you ever cheated on a test or exam?"—from 66 percent in 1981 to 44 percent in 2001.

There is, however, one clear sense in which "cheating" is a significant new problem for Millennials: Neither they nor anyone else seems to able to define the concept as clearly as before. Part of the problem stems from group-oriented changes in pedagogy during the Millennial child era. Compared with 30 years ago, coursework today calls for more collaborative projects, more team studying, more practice quizzes, more take-home essays, and more open-ended problem-solving. Today's college freshmen may be confused about what kind of outside help is allowable. Many high school seniors have college-educated parents who are able and willing to "help a bit" with the occasional college paper, much as they often do with application essays. All of this complicates the very definition of cheating and at some colleges has inspired multi-page memos explaining "allowed" versus "disallowed" practices to students.

The nature of cheating is also complicated by the impact of newly emergent technologies, from on-line digital copying to trading and remixing MP3 music files, all of which blur the distinction between what's original and what's not. For every story we hear about teenagers flocking to HouseOfCheat.com to buy a term paper, we see reports of 30ish entrepreneurs pirating software or 60ish authors (including several best-selling historians) apologizing for "misappropriated" text.

Overall, Millennials are less focused than Boomer collegians used to be on the spontaneous learning experience and more on the bottom-line test result. Many grade school teachers talk about kids who are more knowledgeable but less creative.

There is accordingly some truth to the notion that Millennials are more accepting of imitation, simulation, and condensation than were Boomers and Xers in their youth—and less focused on the personal, the authentic, and the original. In the teen culture others are making for them, Millennials are encountering more remakes of old pop songs and old movies, more infotainment and advertorials that efface the identity of the author, more retro play with yesteryear's pop trends, more willingness to trade, morph, and frame whatever sounds and sights please them. Small wonder that teens show declining interest in who created what, or in how or why they did it.

From the teens' perspective, there is no clear distinction between traditional notions of exam "cheating" and modern notions of information "morphing." Many may see nothing wrong with simply rearranging, in a report or paper, a thought that someone else has expressed with considerable elegance. Some may have a hard time seeing what's wrong with cheating as long as they come up with the right answer, especially if they're employing devices used commonly in business, government, the media—or by professors in their own research.

A special challenge in educating Millennial collegians will be to instill a clear understanding of where originality and plagiarism begin and end—a challenge that in the current cultural and technological environment will require considerable re-thinking and intellectual effort. To make sure students are well versed in the rules, some colleges now require that freshmen take special seminars or sign "integrity contracts." Other colleges are inaugurating or reviving honor codes. Beginning in the fall of 2003, Duke University will require students themselves to enforce a "community standard" for academic honesty. "It's a psychological effect," says Duke President Nannerl O. Keohane. "If people expect you to be honorable, you are more likely to respond with honorable behavior. We have to build a culture where people are genuinely offended by cheating." The success of such efforts may require an institutional willingness to impose the same rules on faculty that are imposed on students.

# 12 | Achieving

"It was one of the few things a high school senior could depend on: Maintain a B+ average and waltz into a major public university. Not any more. These days, even a perfect 4.0 grade-point average doesn't guarantee admission."

— WASHINGTON POST (2000)

# Achieving

Millennials are smart—and getting smarter by the year. They are probably the most all-around capable teenage generation this nation, and perhaps the world, has ever seen. Academics are part of this picture. This year's average national SAT score is the highest since 1974, a 27-year record. And even that achievement understates the trend. Today a much larger share of high-school graduates (just over 45 percent) are taking the exam than took it back in the early '70s (roughly 30 percent)—including millions of poor and nonwhite youths, and the offspring of recent immigrants, who in earlier generations would have been far less likely to take the test.

But academics are hardly the whole picture. When you add their harder-to-measure but just as important accomplishments outside the classroom, the Millennial bottom line is very impressive. In all the talk about how school systems compare around the globe, you never hear about extracurriculars like music, theater, sports, publications, student government, business and prayer clubs, and community service. Nowhere in the world are students doing

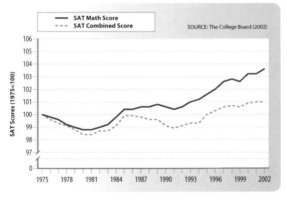

SOURCE: The College Board (2002)

◀ **Figure 21**

Average SAT Scores of Entering College Classes Since 1975 (index, 1975=100)

better in-school work across all these areas than in the United States.

Today's teens know this. They have a high regard for their own generation, which they see as a powerhouse full of high achievers, no matter what some politicians or op-ed writers might say about them. Day to day, it's less a matter of glowing pride than a constant source of personal pressure. One explanation for the continual improvement in behavior, and risk avoidance, of today's teenagers is their anxiety not to fall behind their ever-achieving peers.

More than the Boomers and Gen Xers who preceded them in college, Millennials like large challenges, especially those that require grand constructions such as the building or assembly of material or people. They see their biggest advantages in technology, the economy, and the "social sciences"—rather than in religion or the arts. Surveys confirm that Millennials prefer subjects in which they, and the world, can measure their objective progress. They say they like math and science better than the humanities and arts.

The achievement orientation of Millennials may prove to be the attribute that college officials will like most about this generation. By and large, they are coming to college for the traditional reasons—to learn, to grow, to make new friends, to develop intellectually, to become fully functioning adults. Administrators and faculty who are willing to accept them for what they are will find them, on the whole, to be a delightful group of students.

## Implications for Recruiting and Admissions

Colleges at all levels, all across America, are reporting rises in the quality of applicants and recruits. This is very good news for admissions offices, who might be forgiven their exuberance at basking in the success of their recent recruitment efforts. But when so many colleges report this same result, the conclusion is unmistakable: It's not the new recruitment strategy, it's the pool of students, that is making the difference. According to reports from admissions officers at top colleges, there are now enough high-achieving high school students to fill several Ivy Leagues and still send out rejection notices to plenty of qualified students.

# The Future of Early Decision

......................................

Though "early decision" admissions options date back decades—one of the first "early" plans was instituted by the University of Virginia in 1960—it was not until the late-1990s that these options became a source of heavy admissions pressure on college-bound high school students. The idea really caught on when the most selective colleges began accepting large numbers of early applicants, which had a clear if unintended coercive effect on other colleges.

In 1999, according to NACAC's Admission Trends Survey, 27 percent of responding colleges (and disproportionately the elite colleges) offered early decision plans. In many of these colleges, over half of the freshman class for the fall of 1999 was admitted via early decision or "early action," which amounts to early notification without a binding commitment. Starting with the year 2000's crop of high school seniors—the first Millennials—the issue grew more controversial. It became further complicated in the fall of 2002 by Stanford's and Yale's decision to abandon "early decision" while retaining early action for students who agree not to try early action at any other school.

Why the rise in these "early" plans? One explanation lies in the desire of colleges to increase their "yields" and hence their ratings in annual college-rating guides. But there are, as well, clear administrative advantages to spreading out the admissions process over more of the school year. When some students apply in the fall and others in the winter or spring, high school counselors and registrars, and especially college admissions and financial aid officials, have more time to give individual attention to students. Colleges can manage enrollments more carefully and reduce the uncertainty over the size of each incoming class. Colleges focusing on "enrollment management" also prefer to admit students for whom they are a clear "first choice" and not a backup to somewhere else, and who may be less likely to transfer out after the freshman year.

Early decision is popular among many college applicants too. It allows high school seniors to simplify their college choices, resolve everything early, reduce stress in their senior year (if they get in), and allow themselves "safety net" second chances (if they don't). It has become popular among alumni-child applicants, especially the sons and daughters of wealthy contributors, who use it to take advantage of whatever admissions edge colleges may offer them.

The criticisms of early decision are fourfold:

1. **Accelerated decisions**. Early decision pushes up the student's application deadline by two months—and, implicitly, the acceptance by six months. This, in turn, requires students to do college trips, and take SATs, earlier than they otherwise might.

2. **Senior slump**. High school teachers complain that early-admitted students become less serious about schoolwork in the spring semester of the senior year, and that a split in morale can arise between those students whose fate is settled and those who are still uncertain.

3. **Money and aristocracy**. No question, early decision favors students from wealthy families over those from middle- or low-income families. It boosts the chances of "full-freight" applicants, especially children of wealthy alumni, while adding new financial risks to applicants who will require financial aid, by weakening their bargaining position and preventing them from shopping for affordable colleges.

4. **Shifting the bargaining advantage from student to college**. Viewed as a contract, early decision reverses the order of "offer" and "acceptance" from what it used to be. In the normal spring admissions process, colleges make a binding offer, and then students have about a month to accept. In early decision, students make a binding offer, and then colleges have a month or two to accept. (And, if rejected, a student must often scramble to submit spring applications ahead of January deadlines.)

In the era of the Millennial collegian—with intrusive parents and fresh legions of highly ambitious applicants, all under the glare of the media—every aspect of the college admissions process will be the focus of growing controversy and reform. In the midst of this flux, here's what to expect: First, certain aspects of early decision have such an obvious appeal to Millennials (early planning, long-term commitments, efficient use of time) that some form of this "fast track" process will endure. Second, certain deficiencies of early decision are so glaring that they will be reworked. To prevent "senioritis," senior grades could be made the basis for remedial classes for college freshmen. To protect students in less affluent families, colleges could be required to stipulate financial aid levels in advance. And to equalize bargaining power, the colleges' response period could be shortened, or spring application deadlines extended.

For institutions of higher education, the implications are double-edged. Yes, it means that now is an immensely opportune time for any college to raise its overall academic standing. But it also means that competition between admissions offices will rise as more and more colleges find this out. The college that does not raise its admissions could, in effect, be regarded as falling behind, in relation to its traditional rivals.

To move up a notch, colleges should take care not to trumpet academics above all else. While it is true that Millennials are well-accustomed to the idea that their intellectual worth can be objectively measured, and that those who succeed by such measures should be rewarded, at the same time, Millennials want and need to participate in a strong and diverse community life. It is the challenge of every college to persuade prospects that four years on its campus can shore up their weaknesses (as individuals and as a generation) as well as build on their strengths.

This challenge is not easily met, but every institution of higher learning should strive to find a workable balance, and to avoid admissions policies that could breed resentment and backlash. With eyes on the annual *US News & World Report* "yield" rankings, many colleges are pushing applicants to make binding "early decision" commitments at the start of senior year. And with eyes on their average SAT rankings, many private colleges are offering tuition cash-back discounts (alias "scholarships") to students with scores above a certain level.

Yet it's hardly a success when a college recruits a bright student who has a high probability of transferring out the next year. This is one reason why some schools are explicitly focusing on a less-than-elite clientele, and rejecting applicants who are obviously looking upon them as a "safety" school. They are targeting their marketing to students of an appropriate ability level, neither too high nor too low, and offering these recruits the biggest grants, to achieve a more durable campus community and a higher ratio of graduations.

In recruiting pitches, colleges should tout their infrastructure for student activities, especially for first- and second-year students. Many graduating high-school seniors will have greatly enjoyed their leadership role in the

# The Coming Revolution in Educational Technology

After years of false steps and disappointed predictions, "distance education"—the generic term for learning "at a distance" through new information technologies (IT's)—has finally arrived.

According to International Data Corporation, worldwide revenues in the corporate e-learning market will pass $23 billion in 2004—up from a mere $2 billion in 1999. Two-thirds of current revenues are in North America, and IT accounts for a declining share of the content. By one recent count, colleges in 130 countries now offer over 55,000 courses on line; U.S. colleges alone offer 158 on-line graduate programs. In 2001, Massachusetts Institute of Technology amazed the academic world by announcing "OpenCourseWare," a project that will shortly make all MIT course material available on the Internet, free of charge, to anyone in the world. MIT's declared purpose is to "advance technology-enhanced education" and "to serve as a model for university dissemination of knowledge in the Internet era."

Over the next decade, this technological tide will be surging just as Millennials are passing through college.

As the nation's leading consumers of education, they will play a major role—but what?

Millennials will gravitate easily toward—even insist upon—information technologies that simplify and streamline their educational experience. Fancy gadgets alone won't impress; they will have to work sensibly in a real-world setting.

Because Millennials like to work in teams, a college should pay special attention to technologies that allow students to corroborate on group projects and to create different kinds of "virtual communities" for the purpose of research, experimentation, model building, essay review, and final evaluation. This is how large institutions can replicate some of the advantages of a small college.

Given how highly Millennials are likely to value the best thinkers, lecturers, and data banks in any field, a college can set up high-quality audio and video links to other universities and to research institutes and government agencies the world over. This is how small institutions can duplicate some of the advantages of a large university.

A growing number of colleges, meanwhile, will be tempted to offer on-line a full distance-learning curriculum, complete with programs and degrees. And, notwithstanding MIT's example, most of them will sooner or later expect to generate revenue in the process.

Expect a mixed reaction from Millennial teens and their parents. For the most part, Millennials who go to college yearn for a flesh-and-blood rite of passage, a community of peers who really work and play and live together. This isn't just about knowledge and skills.

There are, however, two subgroups who might be effectively targeted by distance-education programs. First, high-aptitude male teens with a negative attitude about college life might be attracted by the idea of going it alone. They may have no other choice if currently in the military service or otherwise employed. For these males, think of distance education as marketing, since many of them may later apply to come in person. Second, a growing number of affluent students abroad might like an American education but may not have the means or (in an era of tightening visa policies) the opportunity to attend.

arts, or publications, or student government, and they will not look forward to having to wait until their junior or senior year of college to feel the same sense of participation. The more extracurricular facilities a college can tout, the better its chance of attracting and keeping high achieving students.

Millennials take digital technology for granted. To them, laptops and T-1 connections aren't "high tech"; they're just tools that might allow you to better organize society or explore truly new frontiers like nanotechnology or the human genome. Institutions that are paleotech—not wired with powerful intranets, power point tools, and the latest information retrieval systems—will face a real handicap when recruiting students, and not just in technology fields.

## Implications for Campus Life

Millennials are very busy young people, and their quests lie only partly in the classroom. Mirroring what has been happening in high schools recently, they will engage very robustly in all kinds of extracurricular activities. Where the Gen X collegiate era was marked by substantial construction of athletic facilities, colleges would now do well to build other extracurricular infrastructure to match: theaters, music halls, art studios, meeting rooms, student offices—better to make them numerous rather than large, and preferably with cutting-edge technology.

To connect with each other often and to arrive at a campus-wide (or even nationwide) consensus, Millennials will not need big physical structures. With fiberoptic cables in place, they will be able to set up a virtual forum of any size at almost any moment's notice.

Most of today's universities regard themselves as cutting-edge when it comes to technologies. Yet before any university congratulates itself over-much, it ought to compare its progress to the world of the "normal" student of Palo Alto High School, in the heart of Silicon Valley, as profiled in a June 1999 *Wall Street Journal* story:

> *"I've had seven different Power Point presentations," says senior Phil Polansky, referring to a program normally used in business meetings. At another desk, Jennifer Creason talks of pulling three all-nighters in a row to finish a Web page that was part of a physics project.... As with most schools, the athletes are considered the coolest, but at Paly, the hierarchies are in flux. "We're the nerdery, not with the cool kids," says Mr. Polansky, part of the robot [honors-class] crew. "But we're not the lowest. They need us to run the school, since lots of our teachers can't use the technology."*

Colleges need to provide collegians like this with tools, and then let them go to work.

## Implications for the Classroom

While many Boomer and Xer students struggled with mathematics, most Millennials show a better grasp of the topic. Math and science departments can be expected to show the same kind of dynamism and innovation in teaching that humanities experienced during the Boomer student era and business and the arts during the Gen X student era.

Unlike Gen Xers, who came to college with different expectations, Millennials and their parents are accustomed to high academic standards, intense amounts of schoolwork, and strong internal and external pressure to seek out and overcome challenges. Expect students, parents, and public officials to demand higher academic standards, smaller classes, straight forward grading policies that cannot be gamed, and a new Millennial-era mixture of traditional values with cutting-edge technology.

In class, technology should be viewed as an underpinning for every subject that requires it—which, to Millennial eyes, extends to nearly everything. Some faculty members may need remedial tech-ed just to come up to the minimal level that students will expect. While accommodating these tech-adept Millennials, however, do not give in too far to "net thinking." The rising generation of students are so accustomed to doing their research over the Internet that many hardly know their way through library stacks, an old periodical, a microfiche reader, or a great book in its original language—all skills they need to learn.

# 13 | Graduation and Beyond

"Most teenagers are making good
choices—focusing on their futures
and saying no to anything that would
jeopardize their dreams."

— DONNA SHALALA, SECRETARY OF HEALTH AND HUMAN SERVICES (2000)

# Graduation and Beyond

For a generation, as for a person, college is preparation for life. In the fall of 2004, the leading edge cohort of the Millennial Generation will begin graduating en masse from four-year colleges and entering the work force, graduate school, and the ranks of alumni.

As they do, college classrooms will continue to fill with later-wave Millennials, many of whose mentors—from songwriters, movie stars, and athletes to the RA's down the hall in the dorm—will now be the older, cutting-edge members of their own generation.

In several areas, universities would do well to plan ahead for this.

## Post-Graduate Career Services

What will post-graduate placement work be like, two to four years from now? Much depends on the economy, of course, but—viewed purely in terms of generational dynamics—the challenges will become newly daunting. The first job after college will represent, to Millennials and their parents, the initial payoff for all the planning, stress, and shared ambition that will have gone in to these students' first 22 years.

Brace once again for the "helicopter parent," "the team" (consultants, lawyers, assorted other planners), and the media to follow Millennials during and after their senior collegiate year, much as they have up to this point. This means that college career counselors will have more people looking over their shoulders, and feel more pressure to achieve results, than ever before.

Because expectations will have been so high for so long, the odds will seem stacked against the job placement process. Unless the economy is roaring with tremendous force, there will be many students who will have no choice but to scale back their expectations, economic and otherwise. It is already often said that, when a career counselor helps a senior find a good job or graduate school, this is regarded as the student's own success, and when not, as the counselor's own failure. This sentiment will become more widespread in the years ahead when the inevitable setbacks of stressed-out Millennial grads trigger disappointment, even anger, from Boomer parents.

Colleges are acknowledging this by referring to their staff as "career services" rather than "placement" counselors, and by asking those counselors to stress the logistics, timing, and other strategies of the job search process, rather than directly helping students land a job. But that's more a post-Gen X tactical retreat than a Millennial-era advance.

There are three new ways colleges can address the career needs of this new generation.

First, they can try to cultivate among students a sense of perspective about life—a sense that "success," as narrowly defined, may be highly overrated. Many stressed-out students will be very receptive to this message, even as they continue down their high-pressure paths. Counselors can encourage students to broaden their activities beyond coursework, to engage in numerous extracurricular activities (including those in which they may not excel), and to do community service. More concretely, career counselors need to find creative ways to inform Millennials that their ultimate contribution and worth will not be determined by their starting salary, the prestige of their first employer, or the rank of their professional school. With their long time horizons, this is a lesson Millennials will understand—and appreciate.

Career counselors should strive to give every student equal effort and equal care. The winner-take-all, losers-go-fish attitude that Gen Xers tolerated—often by thinking, hey, I can always get a fresh start somewhere else—will be tolerated no longer. It will violate the emerging Millennial team ethic.

Second, college career services should pay close attention to structural labor market trends, identifying sectors with growing job demand and encouraging seniors to plan their lives effectively around the available opportunities.

Recall how, for the past three generations, young adults gravitated to employment bastions that colleges could have foreseen: The graduation of the Silent Generation (the collegians of the '50s and early '60s) coincided with an explosion in what were then called the "helping professions." The graduation of Boomers, in the late '60s and '70s, coincided with a surge in "culture careers"—in marketing, teaching, and the media. The graduation of Gen Xers, in the '80s and '90s, came with a spurt in high-tech entrepreneurial start-ups.

In the coming years, college career services should focus on those opportunities where the Millennial persona will mesh with large new employment demands. Begin by looking at any sector about to experience a massive retirement wave. Large manufacturing corporations are one example. Civil service is another. Of necessity, federal, state, and local governments are about to become major employers of entry-level Millennials. Look also to occupations where demographic and societal trends point to major growth, such as health care, science, the laying out of a new technological infrastructure—and defense, including homeland security.

Third, career services need to pay special attention to the kinds of employers and employment circumstances that will appeal to (and work for) this rising generation. That means employers that can offer teamwork, fairness (equal treatment across broad categories of workers), fewer job definitions, protection against risk, solid work-life balance, longer career plans, and closeness to mom and dad.

In planning new job and career placement strategies, colleges should also keep in mind that the current numerical advantage in female over male grads is likely to continue—though it could be brought quickly back toward parity by a severe economic slowdown, which would make college newly attractive for unemployed men in their twenties.

Thus far, Millennials look to be less entrepreneurial (and risk-taking) than Gen Xers were as young job seekers and job holders, and more likely to engage in longer-range planning. Recent surveys of teenagers show 84 percent saying "security" is very important in future careers, whereas only 26 percent say "owning your own business" is important. Fully 88 percent have "specific" 5-year career goals. Their list of four top work skills are: (1) getting along well with others; (2) working well as part of a team; (3) relating well with people of different races/ethnicities; and (4) being able to use a computer.

To date, reports from employers of summer teen workers (or "interns," as they are increasingly called) have been overwhelmingly positive. According to *American Demographics*, these Millennial attitudes, combined with their on-the-job performance, suggests that "the workplace atmosphere of 2010 could be a much calmer and more low-key place than it is today." Joan Ryan of the *San Francisco Examiner* correctly notes that Millennials "will be more socially adept than Gen Xers and more trusting of institutions, which they see as extensions of parental love and concern, and thus will be more attracted to staying in one job for a long time."

One of the great worries of career counselors, and of parents (if less often of Millennials themselves), is that the graduates of this generation could collide with harsh economic times. If so, many years of test-taking, stressing, and resumé-building would culminate in not just a *generational* disappointment—but a *national* one. A vast army of over-educated under-employed youth is not an outcome older generations will tolerate. In any nightmare economic scenario, the government will step in—coming to the aid of beleaguered college career counselors, with a perhaps "New New Deal" style jobs program. If other generations (like aging Boomers) have to cut back their own benefits to pay for it, so be it.

Depending on the course of the economy, and national security, Millennials may be summoned (or conscripted) to participate in a new national service program. If so, this could fundamentally alter college admissions processes, or career counseling services, or both. Compulsory national service would not add the same stress to campus life that the draft did in the Boomer collegiate era.

## Graduate and Professional Schools

Many of the same trends that are now hitting colleges can be expected to hit graduate schools around the middle of this decade. Universities with large graduate student bodies would be wise to prepare for this.

For the last twenty years, graduate and professional schools have been mostly anonymous Gen X arenas, filled with careerists pursuing scattered business and research niches—young people who have come and gone at different ages with different agendas and who have lived off campus as proto-adults with few ties to the community and unbothered by supervisors or institutional expectations.

All this will change.

In time, graduate and professional school faculties and staffs will see much of what college administrators are already experiencing. Though the reach of parents will fade a bit, given the students' older ages, the tie to mom and dad and family will nonetheless be greater than it is among grad students today. Students will demand more safe and secure facilities and more family-friendly living environments.

When Millennials apply, admissions personnel should brace for over-prepared planners who "chose" their school before even entering college or who took their LSATs or GREs years in advance. To deter premature commitment, some schools might consider requiring all testing and admissions processing to be completed no more than one year prior to the admission filing deadline. College-age Millennials may reach a point of test and application exhaustion, prompting them to vent criticisms about graduate and professional school admissions procedures that, in their view, needlessly add to competitive stress.

To insulate themselves against constant competition from peers, many Millennials with an eye on graduate school will request rules of fair play that preserves some sense of "balanced life"—along with some relief from the academic stress that, by now, they will have endured for nearly twenty years straight.

The media glare will arrive, along with a new emphasis on "standards" and tests. Expect some serious scandals in admissions, financial aid, accreditation, and grad student exploitation (for example, making them toil as minimum-wage *de facto* teachers or lab hands in some extended PhD programs). The recent proliferation of commercial deals—by professors, students, even entire schools—will become newly controversial. The teaching of ethics classes in law and business schools will grow in popularity among students who want to explore the civic and community dimension of their profession.

The rising professional fields will include government (including national intelligence and security), management, engineering, and the applied sciences (including applied social sciences), and military officer training. Declining areas may include finance, theoretical research, and liberal and fine arts in fields where jobs are not widely available.

The preponderance of women now in undergraduate years will continue into the graduate years. As this happens, new gender gaps could arise, notwithstanding any institutional efforts to resist them. The humanities and the "people" professions (law, health care, education) may become increasingly female. Areas like management, science, and technology could remain as male bastions, even as women outnumber men overall. As women come to dominate graduate school life, young women with professional aspirations may also start marrying and giving birth at earlier ages than is now the case. If so, graduate schools will face increasing pressure to accommodate the needs of new mothers.

Graduate and professional schools must brace for the very busy, structured, and connected lives of this generation. Faculties that expect total self-direction and leave their graduate scholars isolated, alone, and drifting for months at a time can expect an unpleasant backlash. Millennials will demand that masters and doctoral programs establish clear time tables and deadlines—binding on both students and professors.

Deepening their quest for the "balanced life," Millennials will also expect something beyond just book time, computer time, and class time during their grad school years. They will demand more opportunities for clinical work, job apprenticeship, and career-related community service. Having been absorbed in extracurriculars throughout their high school and college years, many will also want to pursue activities totally unrelated to their professional training. As Millennials pass through, one can picture law schools forming a women's soccer league, business schools putting on musicals, education schools publishing newspapers, arts academies starting businesses.

## Future Alumni

In all likelihood, Millennials will be an active, loyal, and giving generation of alumni. The early signs—their high level of institutional trust and the respect they show to older people—suggest they will be much more valuable to their colleges over their lifetimes than Boomers or Xers have been or will be. They will take pride in their institutions, in "belonging" to their own special colleges and fraternities and sororities. They will keep in touch with their fellows later in their career lives, return for reunions, and (most important) open their wallets for their alma maters.

By the end of the current decade, expect Millennials to take an active mentoring role with the younger members of their own generation as they enter college in their turn. By then, Millennials will dominate a youth culture that will look very different from the mostly Gen X youth culture of today. What is coming will far more effectively bridge the spectrum of tastes and interests of people in their twenties than is now the case.

For all these reasons, colleges should start now to develop programs to involve Millennials in collegiate affairs. A good way to start is to find new ways of including them in the recruitment and admissions process.

Once students graduate, colleges should plan on treating them like family, using all the Millennials' familiar technologies—combined with old-fashioned homecomings and alumni days—to stay in touch with them through their young adulthood. Outreach efforts that may have seemed like an utter waste of time for Boomers and Gen Xers will, down the road, pay off with Millennials.

# 14 | The Next Great Collegiate Generation

"Every generation has its chance at greatness. Let this one take its shot."

— *NEWSWEEK* (2000)

# The Next Great Collegiate Generation

Every generation has its rags-to-riches success stories of people who raised themselves up from dire circumstances to become business leaders, politicians, or doctors. But with the Millennials, this kind of bootstrapping has become institutionalized, as described by a recent *Wall Street Journal* account of one student's quest for a college education:

> *Lestie Gonzalez grew up poor in New York's south Bronx section. He is dyslexic, and was raised by a single mother who, due to health reasons, could not work to support Lestie and his two younger brothers. His high school was described as "the last stop for students who have been thrown out of other schools." He did not consider attending college until strongly encouraged by a guidance counselor who was placed at his school through a private initiative called College Bound.*
>
> *In the fall of 2002, Lestie, 19, entered Mercy College as a freshman. Mercy College, located just north of New York City, has a program for students with learning disabilities like dyslexia. Lestie's college counselor helped him to navigate the complexities of the Federal and state student aid systems, to enable him to afford higher education.*

Clearly, no other generation has benefited from such an elaborate system of safety nets, individual assistance, and societal expectations. And, just as clearly, Millennials deserve the attention, help, and expectations that adults have showered on them. This is an exceptional generation that is reversing a whole slew of negative societal trends that have had commentators wringing their hands for decades.

In a sense, though, the rise of the Millennials puts greater pressure and responsibility on America's colleges. Greater responsibility, because of the high hopes today's parents are putting in their children. And greater pressure, because today's collegians have extremely high expectations of institutions charged with their education and improvement.

It is not just low-income minority students like Lestie Gonzalez who are showered with attention and care. Across social classes and ethnic groups, Millennial teens and children are protected, lauded, and encouraged to achieve.

For a college or university to be successful today, the administration and faculty must respond to the Millennials' needs, expectations, and aspirations. A college or university that fails to respond will find itself at a disadvantage in recruiting and retaining top students—and will find that students it does recruit will be less likely to perform up to potential.

The potential payoffs are enormous. College life in the Millennial era will be dynamic, energizing, and inspiring. Students will use their drive and energy to help transform and improve not only the campus, but the surrounding community and even the nation through volunteerism and service. They will find new and exciting ways to strengthen campus life, to participate robustly in fine arts, sports, student government, and other extracurricular activities, to enhance the power of technology in education, and to work collectively to solve problems facing the university family.

Millennials are already the most achievement-oriented collegians in our nation's history, and by the time they leave the campus gates, they may be the most learned and capable graduates ever.

As they start graduating from college (2004), professional schools (2006–07), and Ph.D. programs (2008–09), they will fill the ranks of young-adult celebrities in the Olympics, pro sports, and entertainment—and the ranks of the military, in any wars the nation may wage. In 2006, the first Millennials will reach the current median female marriage and childbirth age, in 2009 the median male marriage age. Between around

2007 and 2012, they will make a major mark on the youth pop culture (which until then will remain dominated by Gen X). A new youth activism, of which we will get a solid dose in 2004, will begin having real impact on national politics in the elections of 2008 and 2012.

Through the 2010s, they will be giving birth in large numbers, returning to college for their fifth-year reunions—and swarming into business and the professions, no longer as apprentices. Some will enter state houses and the U.S. Congress. Around 2020, they will elect their first U.S. Senator—around 2030, their first U.S. President. Through the 2020s, their first children will apply to college. They will occupy the White House into the 2050s, during which period they will also provide majorities in the Congress and Senate, win Nobels, rule corporate boardrooms, and fill the ranks of collegiate parent bodies. Thereafter, into the 2070s, they will occupy the Supreme Court, be America's new retirees, and provide academe with its most valuable alumni contributors. Many will still be in their eighties in 2100, some still going on in 2120.

What will happen over the course of their lives is, of course, unknowable. But in all likelihood, the Millennial Generation will dominate the story of the 21st Century in much the same degree as the World War II-winning G.I. Generation dominated the story of the 20th. Will future writers have reason to call them, on their record of achievement, another "great generation"? Time will tell.

Along the way, history will intrude on their lives. This may indeed happen while they are still on campus. When and how, no one can say. Whatever the peril, whatever the challenge—economic, political, military, social, environmental—do not expect years of 1960s-style picketing, protesting, yelling, and arguing. Instead, expect 1930s-style energizing, organizing, teaming, and doing. The graver the national peril, the more Millennials will become the center of attention. What they need will become a national priority. What they do will become a source of national anguish to some, but (let's hope) a source of national pride to most.

If history deals America some bitter challenges—say, a protracted and large-scale War on Terror or a severe economic contraction—young collegians and graduate students may well mobilize to meet the challenge with more optimism and less complaint than older administrators and faculty members.

Millennials will know that the bulk of their lives will lie in the years *beyond* the crisis—whereas the bulk of the faculty lives will have transpired in the years *before* it. And, by nature of their core traits—from their confidence to their team skills to their high-pressure high-achieving frame of mind—they may, as a group, provide just what those times will require.

Millennials will see in such national challenges a lifetime agenda—an agenda very unlike what Boomers set for themselves back in their own youth, or Gen Xers in theirs. Wherever they choose to go, and no matter how difficult the times, colleges and universities may enjoy a new golden age, as they serve this very special generation in what could be uniquely challenging times.

Millennials are rising—and, with them, so may the service to history of higher education.

## About the Authors

Neil Howe and William Strauss, best-selling authors and national speakers, are renowned authorities on generations in America. They have together written four books, all widely used by businesses, colleges, government agencies, and political leaders of both parties. Their blend of social science and history—and their in-depth analysis of American generations—lend order and meaning, even a measure of predictability, to social change.

Their first book, *Generations* (Morrow/Quill, 1991), is a history of America told as a sequence of generational biographies. *Generations* has been photographed on Bill Clinton's desk, publicly praised by House Speaker Newt Gingrich, mailed to every member of Congress by then-Senator Al Gore, and used by pollsters, demographers, and economic forecasters.

Their second book, *13th-Gen* (Vintage, 1993), remains the top selling nonfiction book on Generation X. *The Fourth Turning* (Broadway, 1997) forecast a major mood change in America shortly after the new millennium—a change much like what actually happened, after September 11, 2001. *The Fourth Turning* reached #10 on the amazon.com list four years after its release, and its web site (fourthturning.com) has the internet's longest-running discussion forum for any nonfiction book. "We will never be able to think about history in the same way," declared public opinion expert Dan Yankelovich,

The most recent Howe-Strauss book, *Millennials Rising* (Vintage, 2000), has been widely quoted in the media for its insistence that today's new crop of teens and kids are very different from Generation X and, on the whole, doing much better than most adults think. "Forget Generation

X—and Y, for that matter," says the *Washington Post*, "The authors make short work of most media myths that shape our perceptions of kids these days." According to the *Chronicle of Higher Education*, "Administrators say they can already see indicators of the trends predicted by the authors." The *New York Times* agrees: 'The book is stuffed with interesting nuggets. It is brightly written. And it illuminates changes that really do seem to be taking place." "It's hard to resist the book's hopeful vision for our children and future," adds *NEA Today*. "Many of the theories they wrote about in their two previous books—*Generations* and *13th-Gen*—have indeed come to pass."

Articles by Howe and Strauss have appeared in the *Atlantic*, the *Washington Post*, the *New York Times*, *American Demographics*, *USA Today*, *USA Weekend*, and other national publications.

The Strauss-Howe theories and predictions are based on the authors' profiles of generations—each reflecting distinct values formed during the eras in which its members grew up and came of age. They have observed that similar generational profiles recur in cycles driven by a rhythmic pattern of nonlinear shifts or "turnings" in America's social mood. This cyclical pattern has been present for centuries, and not just in America. History shapes generations, and then generations shape history.

William Strauss is also co-founder and director of the Capitol Steps, a professional satirical troupe that has performed over 7,000 shows, three PBS specials, and fifty radio shows for NPR stations. The Steps have released 22 albums and two books (most recently, *Sixteen Scandals*), and have performed numerous times off-Broadway, often with Strauss in the cast. Strauss has written two musicals, *MaKiddo* (a parody of The Mikado, about gifted teenagers and pushy parents) and *Free-the-Music.com* (about teens who download music and a big music company that wants to stop them). In the summer of 1999, Strauss co-founded the Cappies, a high school "Critics and Awards" program (cappies.com). Through the Cappies, now a nationwide program, high school students attend and review each others' plays and musicals and hold Tonys-style Cappies Galas. A native of San Francisco, Strauss is a graduate of Harvard College (1969), Harvard

Law School (1973), and the Kennedy School of Government (1973). He has four children, aged 18 to 25. His wife Janie serves on the Fairfax County School Board. They live in McLean, Virginia.

Neil Howe is also Senior Advisor on Public Policy to the Blackstone Group and Senior Advisor to the Concord Coalition. He has written extensively on budget policy and aging and on attitudes toward economic growth, social progress, and stewardship. He has drafted several Social Security reform plans and testified on entitlements many times before Congress. In 1996 he drafted the "National Thrift Plan" on which Governor Dick Lamm ran his Reform Party candidacy. He coedits the *Facing Facts* faxletter for the Concord Coalition and coauthors the *Entitlements and the Aging of America* chartbook for the National Taxpayers Union Foundation. Howe grew up in California, took his B.A. at U.C. Berkeley, studied abroad in France and Germany, and later received graduate degrees in economics (M.A., 1978) and history (M.Phil., 1979) from Yale University. He currently lives in Great Falls, Virginia, with his wife, Simona, and two children, aged 8 and 10.

# About LifeCourse Associates

LifeCourse Associates is a generational consulting firm developed by Howe and Strauss in response to the many inquiries resulting from their books. They offer keynote speeches, seminars, communications products, generational audits, and consultations that apply the authors' unique historical analysis to help audiences better understand their businesses, families, and personal futures. Their ideas and generational perspective can have a profound effect on strategic planning, marketing, product development, communications, and human resources.

In recent conferences, both the U.S. Department of Labor and U.S. Department of Health and Human Services have adopted the Howe-Strauss generational framework. Other LifeCourse clients include the Ford Motor Company, Kraft Nabisco, Procter and Gamble, Quest Marketing, PBS, Viacom, AARP, U.S. Marine Corps, U.S. Environmental Protection Agency, Scholastic, Inc., DeMarche Associates, Fleet Street Financial Services, U.S. Bureau of the Census. They have spoken to the faculty and administrators of many colleges and to national collegiate organizations, such as the American Association of Collegiate Registrars and Admissions Officers (AACRAO), the National Association of College Admissions Counselors (NACAC), and the Council of Independent Colleges (CIC).

To contact LifeCourse Associates
call (866) 537-4999
or go to www.lifecourse.com

# Sources

Given the vast range of topics covered in this book—and the innumerable scholarly, journalistic, and pop culture sources that bear some connection to them—there is no way everything of interest can be referenced. Readers who wish to dig deeper into the data sources for the behavior and attitude trends described here should consult the comprehensive bibliographic reference section included at the end of *Millennials Rising* (2001). As a convenience, a brief list of sources (from publications and Websites to programs and agencies) is provided based on what the authors have found useful.

Readers who want to find out more about the authors' generational perspective on American history, or their earlier treatments of the Millennial Generation, are encouraged to read their three previous coauthored books: *Generations* (1991), *13th-Gen* (1993), and *The Fourth Turning* (1997).

Readers with further questions are invited to contact the authors at LifeCourse Associates.

## Sources on Behavior, Summary List

### General

The Child and Family Web Guide (Tufts University), www.cfw.tufts.edu

Child Trends DataBank (Child Trends), www.childtrends.org

*America's Children* (U.S. Federal Interagency Forum on Child and Family Statistics), annual publication

*Trends in the Well-Being of America's Children and Youth* (U.S. Department of Health and Human Services), annual publication

*The State of Children in America's Union* (Children's Defense Fund), annual publication

### Demographics, Family Structure, Race, Ethnicity, Family Income
U.S. Bureau of the Census

### Youth Employment
U.S. Bureau of Labor Statistics (Department of Labor)

### Educational Achievement
National Assessment of Educational Progress, "The Nation's Report Card" (U.S. Department of Education), regular publications, nces.ed.gov/nationsreportcard

The College Board, publications, www.collegeboard.com

### Schools & Colleges
U.S. National Center for Education Statistics, *The Condition of Education* (U.S. Department of Education), published annually, nces.ed.gov

### Children's Use of Time
Sandra L. Hofferth and Jack Sandberg, *Changes in American Children's Time, 1981-1997* (Nov 9, 1998), Institute for Social Research and Population Studies Center, University of Michigan

### Youth Health & Risk Behaviors
U.S. National Center for Health Statistics

U.S. Centers for Disease Control and Prevention

U.S. National Institute of Child Health and Human Development (National Institutes of Health, Department of Health and Human Services)

Youth Studies Group, Stanford Center for Research in Disease Prevention

### Teen Births, Abortions
Alan Guttmacher Institute, publications, www.agi-usa.org

### Youth Sexual Behaviors
Youth Risk Behavior Surveillance System (U.S. Centers for Disease Control and Prevention), www.cdc.gov/nccdphp/dash/yrbs

### Family Dysfunction
U.S. Children's Bureau (Administration on Children, Youth and Families, of the Administration for Children and Families, Department of Health and Human Services)

U.S. National Center on Child Abuse and Neglect (Administration on Children, Youth and Families, of the Administration for Children and Families, Department of Health and Human Services)

### Youth Drug Abuse

U.S. Substance Abuse and Mental Health Services Administration (Department of Health and Human Services), regular publications, www.samhsa.gov

Lloyd D. Johnston, Jerald G. Bachman, and Patrick M. O'Malley (project directors) Monitoring the Future Study, Institute for Social Research, University of Michigan; annual questions to students in grades 12 (since the class of 1975) and in grades 10 and 8 (since the class of 1991); reports issued in various years

Partnership for a Drug Free America, publications, www.drugfreeamerica.org

### Youth Crime

U.S. National Criminal Justice Reference Service (Department of Justice), publications, www.ncjrs.org

National School Safety Center, publications, www.nssc1.org

## Sources on Attitudes, Summary List

### Drexel Poll

Drexel University, *Drexel University Futures Poll: Teenagers, Technology and Tomorrow* (1997)

### Gallup Polls

Gallup News Service, The Gallup Organization (see www.gallup.com)

### Generation 2001

Northwestern Mutual Life, *Generation 2001 Survey* (1999)

### Generational Marketing

*American Demographics* (periodical)

### Horatio Alger

Horatio Alger Association, *The State of Our Nation's Youth*, annual publication, www.horatioalger.com

### Monitoring the Future

Lloyd D. Johnston, Jerald G. Bachman, and Patrick M. O'Malley (project directors) Monitoring the Future Study, Institute for Social Research, University of Michigan; annual questions to students in grades 12 (since the class of 1975) and in grades 10 and 8 (since the class of 1991); reports issued in various years

### NASSP

National Association of Secondary School Principals, *The Mood of American Youth* (1974, 1983, and 1996); students aged 13–17 interviewed early in each year

### Pew Center

The Pew Research Center for the People and the Press, regular published surveys on youth (e.g., *Motherhood Today—A Tougher Job, Less Ably Done*, May 9, 1997)

### Primedia/Roper

PRIMEDIA, Inc., and Roper Starch Worldwide, Inc., *The PRIMEDIA/Roper National Youth Opinion Survey* (1998); students in grades 7–12 interviewed in Nov, 1998

### Public Agenda

Public Agenda, regular published surveys on youth attitudes and adult attitudes toward youth (e.g., *Getting By: What American Teenagers Really Think About Their Schools*, 1997)

### Roper Youth Report

Roper Starch Worldwide, Roper Youth Report; published annually; results reported irregularly (see www.roper.com)

### Shell Poll

Shell Oil Company, *The Shell Poll* (1999)

### TRU

Teenage Research Unlimited, posted news releases, www.teenresearch.com

### UCLA Freshman Poll

L.J. Sax, A.W. Astin, W. S. Korn, and K.M. Mahoney, *The American Freshman* (Higher Education Research Institute, University of California at Los Angeles), published annually, yearly surveys since 1966

### Who's Who

Who's Who Among American High School Students, *Annual Survey of High Achievers*. "High-achieving" high school student interviewed annually since 1967; www.eci-whoswho.com

### YATS

Defense Manpower Data Center, *Youth Attitude Tracking Survey* (U.S. Department of Defense); survey of potential high school-aged recruits; published annually